THE COFFEE COMPANION

~

THE COFFEE COMPANION

~

THE CONNOISSEUR'S GUIDE
TO THE WORLD'S BEST BREWS

JON THORN

RUNNING PRESS
PHILADELPHIA • LONDON

9 8 7 6 5 4 3 2 1

Digit on the right indicates the number
of this printing.

Library of Congress
Cataloging-in-Publication Number
94-73884

ISBN 1-56138-522-0

This book was designed and produced by
Quintet Publishing Limited
6 Blundell Street
London N7 9BH

Creative Director: Richard Dewing
Designer: Ian Hunt
Project Editor: Laura Sandelson
Editor: Lydia Darbyshire
Photographer: Paul Forrester
Illustrator: Katy Sleight

Typeset in Great Britain by
Central Southern Typesetters, Eastbourne
Manufactured in Singapore by
Bright Arts Pte. Ltd.
Printed in Singapore by
Star Standard Industries Pte. Ltd.

This book may be ordered by mail from the publisher.
Please add $2.50 for postage and handling.
But try your bookstore first!

Running Press Book Publishers
125 South Twenty-second Street
Philadelphia, Pennsylvania 19103-4399

CONTENTS

Coffee is the common man's gold, and like gold,
it brings to every man the feeling of luxury
and nobility.

ABD-AL-KADIR (1587)

When you are worried, have trouble of one sort
or another — to the coffee house!

PETER ALTENBERG (1922)

Complacencies of the peignoir, and late
Coffee and oranges in a sunny chair,
And the green freedom of a cockatoo
Upon a rug mingle to dissipate
The holy hush of ancient sacrifice.

"Sunday Morning"
WALLACE STEVENS (1923)

I have measured out my life with coffee spoons.

from "The Love Song of J. Alfred Prufrock"
T. S. ELIOT (1917)

Interior of a café at Constantinople.

*Coffee seeds growing in
a nursery in Brazil.*

THE STORY OF
COFFEE

THE SECRET SPREADS

The coffee plant originated in Ethiopia and the Horn of Africa, where it grows wild even today, but it was in the country now known as Yemen (formerly called Arabia), that the diffusion and horticultural propagation of coffee began. In those days Yemen was one of the busiest places in the world and its main port, Mocha, was its center.

Some authorities say that the cultivation of coffee began in Yemen in A.D. 575, but it was certainly highly developed there by the 15th century, and it was from there that coffee began its great journey around the world. Just as tea was a jealously guarded commodity in China, so was coffee regarded by the Arabs. Coffee beans are the seeds of the coffee plant; when stripped of their outer cherry and husk, they become infertile, and it was only in this form that they were allowed to be exported from Arabia.

Coffee's path from Arabia mirrors to some extent the route that tradition claims coffee followed to arrive in Arabia in the first place. One story tells how black Sudanese slaves were brought through Ethiopia *en route* to Arabia. They took with them supplies of coffee, still in its red cherry coverings, to help them survive the journey, and it was in this way that coffee cherries were carried to Arabia.

It was inevitable that travelers to Mecca, at the heart of the Muslim world, would carry some of the beans with them. One legend recounts that the Arabs themselves took coffee to Sri Lanka (previously Ceylon) as early as 1505, but the man most widely credited with spreading coffee to the East is one Baba Budan, who returned from pilgrimage to Mecca to his home in southwestern India with some fertile beans at some point in the 17th century.

By the early 17th century, German, French, Italian, and, especially, Dutch traders were vying with each other to introduce coffee to their overseas colonies. The Dutch won in 1616 when a coffee plant was taken via Mocha to the Netherlands, and by 1658 the Dutch had started the serious cultivation of coffee in Ceylon (now Sri Lanka).

In 1670 one of coffee's great failures occurred. Some French optimists, who had somehow obtained several plants, attempted to establish a plantation near Dijon, an area notable for its cold winters and freezing fogs. We shall never know why this group thought that plants that prospered in Arabia, and which could be grown in the Netherlands only in heated glasshouses, would flourish in open fields in central France.

One of the key figures in the history of coffee is the Burgermaster of Amsterdam, Nicolaas Witson. In 1696 Witson suggested to Adrian van Ommen, the commander at Malabar, that coffee be taken to Java, then a Dutch possession, and seeds were therefore planted at the Kedawoeng Estate, Batavia. Unfortunately, the seedlings were washed away, but in 1699 Henricus Zwaaydecroon took cuttings from Malabar to Java, and these were successfully transplanted. Thus began the first European plantation, and the profits it quickly brought encouraged others.

In 1706 the first samples of Java coffee and a Javan coffee plant were sent to Amsterdam where the plant was nurtured in botanical gardens. Seeds from the plant were generously distributed to horticultural enthusiasts throughout Europe. Meanwhile, the Dutch were expanding production into Sumatra and the Celebes in the Indonesian archipelago, and Indonesia was the world's first commercial exporter of coffee. Today it is the fourth largest producer and exporter.

Attempts to transfer coffee plants between the Netherlands and France failed until, in 1714, a tree 5 feet tall was sent from Amsterdam to King Louis XIV of France. This tree, which was transferred to the Jardin des Plantes in Paris, is the identifiable ancestor of all the first coffee plants grown in most of the French colonies, and in South and Central America and the Caribbean. In 1715, for example, coffee plants were taken to the Island of Bourbon (now known as La Réunion) and soon the island begun to export coffee.

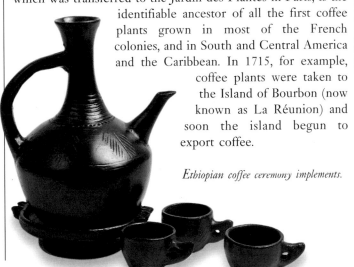

Ethiopian coffee ceremony implements.

GABRIEL MATHIEU DE CLIEU

One of the most romantic of the stories associated with coffee is that of Gabriel Mathieu de Clieu, a French naval officer serving in Martinique. While he was on leave in Paris, de Clieu succeeded in obtaining some plants which he determined to take back to Martinique. This may have been in 1720 or in 1723; or he may have made the journey twice because the first consignment died. What is certain is that de Clieu eventually set sail from Nantes with the most famously and best cared for plant of all time. The plant was stowed on deck in a glass box to protect it from salt spray and to keep it warm.

De Clieu's journal tells how the ship was threatened by pirates from Tunis and how it survived a violent storm. It also reveals that de Clieu had an enemy on board who was jealous of his mission and tried to sabotage the plant, even tearing off

Gabriel Mathieu de Clieu on board a ship bringing the first coffee plant to Martinique.

a branch in one struggle. Then the ship was becalmed and drinking water became short. The selfless de Clieu shared his own ration with the plant.

Finally de Clieu arrived safely in Martinique, and the coffee tree was planted at Prechear, surrounded by thorn bushes and kept under round-the-clock watch by slaves. It thrived and multiplied, and by 1726 the first harvest was gathered. We are told that by 1777 there were 18,791,680 coffee plants on Martinique, from where plants were sent to Haiti, Santo Domingo, and Guadeloupe.

De Clieu did not live to see this triumph. He died in Paris, an honored if not a wealthy man, on November 30, 1724, at the age of 88. He is commemorated by a memorial, which was erected in 1918 in the botanical garden of the Fort de France on Martinique.

COFFEE TRAVELS EAST AND WEST

It was not until 1718, when the Dutch took plants to Surinam on the northeastern coast of South America, that coffee arrived in what quickly became the coffee center of the world. There soon followed the establishment of the first plantation in Para, Brazil, in 1727, with plants from French Guiana. These were followed by a different variety, from Goa, which were planted around Rio de Janeiro. In 1730 the British introduced coffee to Jamaica, initiating the long and fascinating history of Jamaican Blue Mountain coffee. Then, between 1750 and 1760, coffee was first grown in Guatemala. In 1779 Don Francisco Xavier Navarro took plants from Cuba to Costa Rica, and in 1790 coffee was first grown in Mexico. In 1825 seeds from the plantation around Rio de Janeiro were taken to Hawaii, where coffee is grown today – the only genuine U.S. coffee.

In 1878 the story came almost full circle when the foundations of the Kenyan coffee industry were laid by British settlers who introduced coffee plants to British East Africa, which were augmented in 1901 by plants from La Réunion. In 1887 the French established a plantation in Tonkin (now Vietnam), and in 1896 coffee trees were planted in Queensland, Australia.

Thus, the secret that the Arabs had so long sought to keep to themselves was known throughout the world.

11

THE FIRST COFFEE HOUSES

The earliest coffee drinkers are not known to us, but it is almost certain that they lived in Ethiopia. References to a beverage known as "buncham," that may or may not be coffee, are found in Arabic scientific documents dating from A.D. 900–1000, although these are largely interested in the scientific qualities of the bean.

In addition to describing the benefits to "the stomach, the members, the skin," the writers also note that the drink gives "an excellent smell to the whole body," and it is true that coffee does have this unusual quality of appearing to retain its aroma through the sweat glands. In the days before baths were taken regularly and in areas where water was a scarce resource, this deodorant effect must have been greatly appreciated.

An Arab legend, dating from *c.* 1250, relates that the exiled Sheikh Omar discovered coffee berries growing wild. Hungry and bored with eating the raw beans, the sheikh is said to have boiled some of the berries and to have drunk the resulting brew. Not only was this a welcome change in the sheikh's diet, but he also administered the liquid to some infirm people who recovered. The sheikh returned home in triumph from his exile in Mocha – carrying some of the

Painting c. 1910, *Café Turk at Constantinople.*

precious beans with him. There are several versions of this tale, and almost the only element they have in common is the name Omar. Other variants include ghosts; the curing of the beautiful daughter of the king of Mocha; and the ravishing song of a wondrous bird, which disappeared after leading Omar to a tree laden with coffee fruits.

One of the most common legends is that of a goatherd in Arabia – or possibly Egypt or even somewhere else entirely – who noticed that his goats became livelier after eating coffee berries. He reported his findings to the local abbot, who experimented on his monks, and they found that the brew helped them stay awake throughout their nightly prayers.

In the last 200 years, researchers into the origins of coffee have come to some curious conclusions. One writer believes that coffee existed in the time of Homer and that it was drunk at Troy, having been the "wondrous drink" that Helen took with her from Sparta to Troy. Yet another writer has concluded that King David received coffee from Abigail and that both Esau and Ruth drank it.

It is recorded that in 1454 the Mufti of Aden visited Ethiopia and saw his own countrymen drinking coffee there. When he returned home, he sent for some beans, and not only did the beverage cure him of an affliction, but the Mufti also appreciated its ability to keep him awake. It quickly became popular with the dervishes.

Coffee drinking and cultivation in what we now know as Yemen certainly predated 1454. In that year it was approved by the government, which may have felt that the invigorating qualities of coffee were preferable to the soporific qualities of qat (or kat), which was widely grown and used throughout the country.

It was in Mecca that the first coffee houses, known as Kaveh Kanes, were established, and although they were originally religious in purpose, they quickly developed into centers of chess, gossip, singing, dancing, and music. From Mecca they spread to Aden, Medina, and Cairo.

Coffee was taken to Constantinople in 1517 after Salim I had conquered Egypt. From there, the habit of coffee drinking spread throughout the area, becoming established in Damascus by 1530 and in Aleppo by 1532. Two of the best-known coffee houses in Damascus were the Café of the Roses and the Café of the Gate of Salvation.

*Café Florian in the Piazza San Marco, Venice,
is the oldest surviving coffee house in Europe.*

Although coffee houses were not seen in Constantinople until 1554, they were soon famous for their luxurious furnishings, owners vying with each ·other to attract customers. They became meeting places for both social and business reasons and, increasingly, as the home of political debate and dissent. At various times coffee was banned – at one stage, second offenders were sewn into a leather bag and thrown into the Bosphorus – but its respectability was assured when it became subject to tax.

It is easy for us to forget why coffee houses proved to be so popular both in the Middle East and Europe. Quite simply, nothing like them had ever existed before. Before the advent of the coffee house, there had been nowhere to enjoy a pleasant, relatively inexpensive drink in convivial company.

Coffee finally arrived in Europe in 1615, having been brought by Venetian traders. This was several years later than tea, which was first sold in Europe in 1610, and many years after cocoa, which was brought from the New World by the Spanish in 1528.

When coffee was first seen in Italy, some clerics suggested that it should be excommunicated because it must be the devil's work. The pope, Clement VIII (1592–1605), decided to see for himself, and he enjoyed the cup so much that he declared instead that "coffee should be baptized to make it a true Christian drink."

Initially, coffee was regarded as a medicine, and it commanded a high price. It was also largely sold by lemonade vendors. As far as can be determined, the first coffee house – *bottega del caffè* – was opened in Venice in 1683, although one, unsubstantiated, claim suggests that it was 1645. Café Florian in the Piazza San Marco, one of the best-known and, outside Japan, most expensive coffee houses in the world, was opened by Floriano Francescari in 1720. Italian coffee houses are still called *caffès*; elsewhere in Europe they are called *cafés*.

Thereafter, coffee houses proliferated throughout Italy, although most were in Venice. Georgio Quadri, the first owner to offer authentic Turkish coffee, opened his coffee shop in 1775, and this was quickly followed by Duc di Toscania, Imperatore Imperatrice della Russia, Tamerlano, Fantae di Diana, Dame Venete, Pace, and Arabo-Piastrelle.

The first coffee house in England was opened not in London but in Oxford, in 1650 by a man called Jacob. About four years later, a second coffee house, Cirques Johnson, was also opened in Oxford, according to some sources, also by a man called Jacob. A coffee club started in a private house near to All Souls' College later became the Royal Society.

The first coffee house in London was opened in 1652. It was in St. Michael's Alley, Cornhill, and was owned by Pasqua Rosee, who may have been Greek, and a Mr. Bowman. This became the model for many of the coffee houses that subsequently opened, one of the best known of which was Mol's Coffee House in Exeter, Devon. Sir Walter Raleigh used to drink coffee and smoke his pipe there.

IL CAFFÈ DI VENEZIA

Florian

1720

CAFFÈ MACINATO

Café Florian's house coffee.

The most famous survivor of all the London coffee houses was founded, originally in Tower Street and later in Lombard Street, by Edward Lloyd (d. 1730) in 1688. As a service to his customers, Lloyd used to prepare lists of the ships that his clients had insured, and eventually Lloyd's became the largest single insurance house in the world.

The first reference to coffee in North America dates from 1668, when it is described as being drunk with sugar or honey and cinnamon. Soon after this, however, coffee houses were established in New York, Philadelphia, and Boston and other towns.

In Boston the two earliest were the London Coffee House and the Gutteridge Coffee House, which opened in 1691, and one of the most famous was the Green Dragon, where the Boston Tea Party was planned in 1773. Boston was also the site of the largest, most expensive, and grandest coffee-exchange house in the world when, in 1808, a seven-story building, costing $50,000, was built on the model of Lloyd's of London. It was destroyed by fire only 10 years later.

In New York, where coffee quickly replaced "must" (a kind of beer) as the main breakfast drink, the main market for green beans was established in 1683. William Penn sent his orders for beans from Pennsylvania to New York. The first coffee house to be seen in the city was the King's Arms, which was opened in 1696. This was followed by the Exchange Coffee House in Broad Street, which was built in 1730 and became a major trading center. The Exchange was, however, eclipsed by the Merchants' Coffee House, and it was here that the Bank of New York was formed in 1784 and where the first stocks were sold in 1790. The Tontine, on Wall and Water Streets in New York, was the headquarters of the New York Stock Exchange for 10 years.

In Philadelphia, the third great city of early American history, the first coffee house was opened in 1700 – it was simply called Ye Coffee House, and its main competitor was the London Coffee House.

Coffee houses in America differed from their European counterparts, tending to be centers for conservative elements rather than for radicals, republicans or the literati. They also often served as the venue for trials and council meetings in cities where there were few civic buildings.

WHAT IS COFFEE?

Our word "coffee" comes from the Latin name of the genus *Coffea*. The genus is a member of the Rubiaceae family, which includes over 500 genera and 6,000 species, most of which are tropical trees and shrubs.

The 18th-century Swedish botanist, Carolus Linnaeus, described the genus, but botanists are still not in complete agreement on the precise classification. There are probably at least 25 major species within the genus, all indigenous to tropical Africa and some islands in the Indian Ocean, but problems have arisen because of the wide variations that occur in the plants and seeds. All species of *Coffea* are woody, but they can be small shrubs or tall trees more than 32 feet high. The leaves range in color from yellowish to purple.

Botanical drawing of coffee.

From the coffee drinker's point of view, there are two major and two lesser species within the genus. *Coffea arabica*, which Linnaeus identified in 1753, gives us arabica beans, the quality coffee of the world and the only coffee to be drunk on its own, un-blended. Arabica coffees are described either as "Brazils," which come from Brazil, and "Other Milds," which come from elsewhere. *Coffea canephora* or, more accurately, *C. canephora* var. *robusta*, provides the robusta beans, which are often used to make arabica go further. The two minor species within the genus are *C. liberica* and *C. excelsa* (*C. dewevrei*), which give liberica and excelsa beans respectively.

The two best-known varieties of *C. arabica* are Typica and Bourbon, but many strains have been developed, including Caturra (which is grown in Brazil and Colombia), Mundo Novo (also from Brazil), Tico (which is widely grown in Central America), San Ramon (a dwarf strain), and, perhaps most famous, Jamaican Blue Mountain. The average arabica

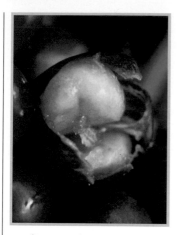

Split cherry showing the beans.

plant is a large bush with dark-green, oval leaves. The fruits are also oval and usually contain two flattish seeds. When only one bean develops, it is known as a peaberry.

The term "robusta" is actually derived from the most widely grown variety of *C. canephora*. It is a robust shrub or small tree that grows to 32 feet or more in height, but it has a shallow root system. The fruits are round and take up to 11 months to mature. The seeds are oval and somewhat smaller than the arabica beans. Robusta coffee is grown in West and Central Africa, throughout Southeast Asia and, to some extent, in Brazil, where it is known as Conilon.

Liberica coffee trees grow strong and tall, to 60 feet in height. They have large, leathery leaves, and the fruits and beans are also large. Liberica coffee is grown in Malaysia and West Africa, but only very small quantities are produced because demand for its individual flavor is low.

At present, arabica coffee represents around 70 percent of the world's production, but the proportion of robusta is increasing, largely because of the better yields that are possible from robusta trees. In addition, arabica trees are more prone to disease than plants producing robusta beans.

Both arabica and robusta trees produce a crop 3–4 years after planting, and they are viable for between 20 and 30 years, depending on conditions and care. Thereafter, they must be replaced. Both species require good amounts of sun and rain. Arabica trees prefer a seasonal climate with a temperature range of 59–75°F; robusta prefers warm, equatorial conditions with more constant temperatures of between 75–85°F. Both species die when the temperature falls below freezing, although the arabica trees are hardier, and both require an annual rainfall of about 60 inches.

The traditional way to grow coffee trees is to grow suitable trees nearby to shade the coffee trees and developing fruit

───── ELEPHANT BEANS ─────

HOWEVER DIFFERENT THE flavors of the various straight original coffees from around the world may be, and whether they are robusta or arabica beans, they are all more or less the same size. There is an exception, however, and that is the elephant bean, which is a third or more larger than other coffee beans. The official name is the *Maragogype*, which derives from the Maragogype County in Bahia state, Brazil, where the bean was first identified in 1870. It is a hybrid of arabica, and once it had been identified and isolated, it quickly proliferated commercially. In 1883 an example found its way to Kew Gardens in Britain, where it thrived. France was an early market for the bean, and before World War I it had achieved such a reputation in Germany that it was the only coffee served in the Kaiser's household.

The *Maragogype* was planted in coffee-producing areas around the world, although today it is produced only in Guatemala, Mexico, Nicaragua, Honduras, El Salvador, Brazil, and Zaire. The best elephant beans are grown in Mexico and Guatemala, and good-quality Zairan beans are becoming increasingly rare. In fact, production worldwide has been falling from a peak reached in the first two decades of this century.

In terms of taste, many people find a lot to admire in a cup of Mexican or Guatemalan elephant beans. It has a balanced flavor: there is no bitterness and a light acidity; the taste is nicely rounded with a little fruit; and there is a very pleasing general smoothness to it.

FROM LEFT: Kenyan Peaberry, MARAGOGYPE (elephant bean), and Kenyan AA.

Aerial view of a coffee plantation in Colombia

from the hottest sun. In addition to limiting the damage that may be caused by direct sun, the trees help to conserve the moisture in the soil. A more modern technique is to use irrigation and fertilizers, which require investment and which must, therefore, be economic in terms of yield and added value, so they are really only viable in commercial plantations.

Coffee is grown on very large estates and in the smallest of forest clearings, and on almost every size of farm and smallholding between. In Brazil and Guatemala, for example, there are many large estates devoted to growing nothing but coffee, and in Brazil in particular mechanical harvesters are increasingly used. The large estates can produce high yields, but they also have high input and capital costs; smaller farms have lower yields but lower costs.

The main variables in coffee production are the labor and land costs. Higher labor costs can be offset by using modern techniques, including the use of fertilizers, herbicides and pesticides, mechanization, and irrigation. But all these methods require investment.

HARVESTING THE BEANS

After 3–4 years, when they come to maturity, the trees bear fruit, which are borne in lines or clusters along the branches of the trees.

The beans that we see are, of course, the seeds of the coffee tree. The seeds are surrounded by a fruit or cherry, which turns red when it is ready to be harvested. Beneath the red skin, the exocarp, there is a fleshy pulp, the mesocarp, then a slimy layer, then a parchment-like covering of the bean, the endocarp. Inside these layers are, usually, two beans, flat sides facing each other, and the beans are covered in a thin membrane or coat.

The berries, or the cherries, as they are usually known, ripen to a bright, lustrous red. Most arabica cherries ripen after 6–8 months; robusta beans take 9–11 months. There can, therefore, really be only one harvest a year, although in countries in which the division between the wet and dry seasons is not clearly defined – Colombia and Kenya, for example – there may be two flowerings a year, therefore permitting a main and a secondary crop.

Harvest times vary, of course, according to geographical zone. North of the Equator – in Ethiopia and Central America, for instance – the harvest takes place between

Green coffee cherries, Brazil.

High bush pickers, East Java, Indonesia

September and December. South of the Equator – in Brazil and Zimbabwe, for example – the main harvest is in April or May, although it may last until August. Equatorial countries – such as Uganda and Colombia – can harvest fruit all year round, especially if plantations take advantage of different altitudes. It is possible, therefore, for there to be freshly harvested beans for much of the year.

The harvesting itself can be done in one of two ways. The first is strip picking, in which the entire crop is picked in one pass through the plantation. The other method, selective picking, involves making several passes at intervals of 8–10 days among the trees so that only the red, fully ripe berries are taken. Selective picking is, clearly, more expensive and labor intensive than strip picking, and it is only employed for arabica beans, especially if those beans are to be wet processed (see page 25).

The number of cherries picked will be determined by a variety of factors, the most obvious of which are the size of the trees and the layout of the farm or plantation. On an average farm, an average picker would probably gather between 100 and 200 pounds of cherries a day. Of this total weight, however, only 20 percent is actually bean, so an average picker would pick 20 to 45 pounds. Coffee is supplied in standard bags of 100 or 130 pounds. Therefore, it takes one picker three to six days to fill one bag.

It is estimated that the costs of harvesting represent about half the total annual costs of a coffee plantation or farm. In Brazil, attempts have been made to reduce these costs by introducing mechanical pickers, which straddle the coffee trees and shake the branches so that the loose, ripe berries fall into hoppers. Mechanical harvesters are only suitable on soft, unchallenging terrain, and they require preplanning, for they are useful only where the trees are planted in straight lines. A mechanically harvested crop will also need to be screened to remove the leaves and twigs that fall into the hopper.

The vast majority of coffee is, therefore, harvested by hand. This results in intensely seasonal work, and the pickers have also to be aware that immature, diseased, or overripe cherries should be avoided, as they will affect the quality of the rest of the crop. Sacks of beans that have been contaminated in some way are described as "common," "sour," or "fermented," the last condition being the worst.

Basket of ripe cherries, East Java.

PROCESSING THE BEANS

There are two ways of preparing coffee beans for roasting, and the method used has a significant effect on the price and quality of the final beans. The cheapest process is known as the "dry" method, which is used for lower-grade beans; the better-quality beans are processed by the "wet" methods.

The dry method is used for "naturals" or unwashed coffee; the wet method is for fully washed or semiwashed beans. Most arabica beans are wet processed, except those from Brazil and Ethiopia, where the dry method is more usual. In Indonesia some robusta beans are wet processed, although this is unusual.

THE DRY METHOD

The dry method of processing coffee is the simplest, cheapest, and most traditional. The harvested cherries are spread over a concrete, brick, or matting surface, ideally in sunlight, and the cherries are raked over at regular intervals to prevent fermentation. If it rains or if the temperature falls, the cherries have to be covered for protection.

After about four weeks, when the moisture content of each cherry will have fallen to about 12 percent, the cherries are dry. (In Brazil at this stage, they are called, somewhat

Drying coffee cherries, Pirajui, Sao Paulo, Brazil.

confusingly, *coco*.) By now, the outer shell will have become dark brown and brittle, and you can actually hear the beans rattling around inside the husk.

This process requires more skill than is apparent, for it is possible to over-dry the beans; if that happens, they are more likely to be damaged during the next stage, hulling. At the same time, beans that are not sufficiently dry are more susceptible to fungal attack. The dried cherries are then stored in silos for a while, during which time the green beans continue to lose moisture.

Old depulping machine, Costa Rica.

THE WET METHOD

The wet process requires greater investment and more care, but it helps to preserve the intrinsic qualities of the bean and causes less damage. The main difference between the two methods is that in the wet method the pulp is removed from the bean almost immediately, instead of allowing the cherries to dry.

The pulp is removed in a pulping machine, which crushes the cherries, either between one fixed and one moving surface or in a machine with adjustable blades. In order to preserve the quality of the beans, pulping has to be done as soon after harvesting as possible – certainly no longer than 24 hours, although before 12 hours have elapsed is ideal. If the beans are left for too long, the pulpy flesh becomes more difficult to separate from the beans, leading to imperfect separation and possible damage to the bean.

The beans, now in their husks, are separated from the skin and pulp, which are washed away with water. The washing channels are designed to separate the lighter, immature beans from the heavier, mature ones, although this separation can also be achieved by means of an Aagaard pre-grader. Aagaard was a Norwegian coffee grower who, when working in Kenya, devised a system involving shaking the beans through a strainer into a tank of water. The larger, heavier beans sink through the water first; the lighter beans are carried further along into the tank. The water in this process can be recycled.

The next stage is the essential fermentation − that is, the separation of the slippery mucilage covering the parchment by the action of enzymes. The beans are stored in fermentation tanks for between 12 and 36 hours, depending on the ambient temperature, the thickness of the layer of mucilage, and the enzymes present. When the process is complete, the parchment surrounding the bean is no longer slimy but has a "pebbly" feel.

Quality control throughout the wet method is essential to prevent a "stinker" bean developing. Even one bean that has been allowed to rot can ruin a whole consignment. For this reason all the equipment used is cleaned daily to guarantee nothing is left before the next batch is processed.

DRYING THE BEANS

The beans are still in their parchment casing, and after the wet method of processing, these casings contain about 50 percent moisture. The parchment has to be dried to about 11 percent moisture so that the beans can be stored in a stable condition. This degree of moisture is critical, because if arabica beans are over-dried to 10 percent, they lose their blue-green color and some quality.

The parchment is dried by spreading the beans on concrete or paved floors or on drying tables or trays, as for the dry method. Mechanical driers are available and are used on some of the larger plantations or where rain could spoil the drying. The beans are placed in conditioning bins, and dry air is blown over them. Otherwise, the drying is left to the sun. The beans are turned regularly to make sure that they dry evenly, and the process takes 12–15 days. It is important that the parchment does not crack, so if the sun is too strong, the beans have to be covered.

Drying coffee beans on racks, Kenya.

At this stage the processing is complete, and the beans are known as "parchment coffee." Ideally, they will remain in this form until immediately before export.

Because producing countries need to export throughout the year and not just in the three or so months of the harvesting period, the coffee is stored as "parchment coffee" in an absolutely stable atmosphere. High humidity is the enemy of coffee, and a humidity of 70 percent could easily damage the beans. For this reason, "parchment coffee" is often not stored on the farms that produced it, although in some areas there may be no alternative. High-grown coffee should be stored at the same or a similar altitude as that at which it was grown because it is particularly susceptible to humidity. Arabica beans in this condition should not be stored for more than 12 months; robusta beans can be stored for a little longer.

MILLING OR HULLING

Just before it is exported, the coffee will be "cured" by milling, which means that the parchment is removed – from both arabica and robusta beans – and the beans are prepared for sale. This removal of the parchment from washed coffee and the remaining outer layers from dry-processed beans is also known as hulling or peeling.

Sewing coffee bags, Brazil

It is more difficult to remove the parchment from wet-processed coffee than from dry-processed beans, and different hullers are used. There are two main types – friction hullers and impact hullers. Friction hullers of the Engelberg or Africa type can process both wet and dry beans. These have a cylindrical casing, and the beans are squeezed between a wire rib and a knife, which shatters the shells, so releasing the beans.

Parchment beans are usually hulled on Smout friction hullers. Jules Smout, a Belgian citizen of Scottish descent who was born in Koenigsberg, Prussia, settled in Guatemala, where, in 1844, he patented a peeler consisting of a rotor with a helical pitch, which turns inside a casing that has spirals turning in the opposite direction to the rotor. The parchment is ground off the beans as they are forced along the rotor. Because it turns relatively slowly, the rotor generates less heat than other types of huller.

Other hulling methods include the roll huller, which is used mainly in South America on dried cherries, and the crossbar huller, which has an internal arrangement of knives.

Impact hullers, which, except in Brazil, are used only for parchment coffees, do not use friction to separate the bean from the parchment. The coffee must have the correct moisture content or the beans will break. The hullers consist of a horizontal disk spinning in a circular chamber. Around the edge of the disk are steel pins or bars, and the beans are forced into contact with the pins by centrifugal force. The parchment shells shatter on contact.

POLISHING

Any silver skin that remains on the beans after hulling is removed by polishing. Most polishing machines work on a similar principle to the Smout huller, but instead of steel they have bronze bars, which do less damage to the beans. The bronze also gives the beans an attractive bluish hue. Beans milled by an impact huller are usually polished because they often look messier than friction-hulled beans.

Historically, polished beans were considered superior to unpolished ones, but there is, in fact, little difference in the resulting cup. The reverse snobbery, that polishing detracts from the cup by over-refining the bean, is sometimes voiced, but the evidence in the cup is doubtful.

GRADING AND SORTING

Beans are graded first by size and then by density. With two exceptions, all coffee beans are of a fairly uniform size and with the same proportions – they are flat on one side and half-oval on the other, and they are longer than they are wide. The exceptions are the peaberry, which is more oval in shape, and the elephant bean or *Maragogype*, which is naturally larger. Both beans often command premium prices.

On the whole, larger beans produce better coffee. Size is expressed on a scale of 10 to 20, although some national quality grades are equivalent to size – Grade AA, for example. The beans are sized by being passed through a strainer, but at this stage even beans of the same size can have different weights, and the containers of beans will include damaged and shriveled beans, which must be removed.

The best way to separate the unwanted beans from the rest is to use gravity and air. The pneumatic method, a highly skilled process, which is done by hand, uses an air jet to separate heavy and light beans. In an alternative method,

gravimetric separators hold the beans on elevated trays, and air is passed up and through them, which causes the heavier beans to fall. This, too, is a highly skilled operation, and when it is carried out properly, it allows more effective and uniform separation.

The next stage is to sort the beans to remove the stinkers, blacks, sours, and foxes and any over-fermented or unhulled beans. This is usually done by eye, with the beans carried along a belt.

Other methods include electronic color sorting, which is mainly used with robusta beans, and the bichromatic method, which uses light to detect "wrong" beans. To date, however, the best sorter is still the human eye, although no doubt microprocessing and high-tech systems will eventually take over this stage completely.

Sorting coffee beans, Bali.

Grading coffee beans, Colombia.

Different countries grade their beans according to different systems. Some of these, like that used in Haiti, are over-complex and pointless. The system used in Brazil, on the other hand, is complex but necessary. In general, however, there are six export grades, the top grade being SHB (strictly hard bean) or strictly high grown, which indicates that the beans were produced at a minimum altitude, 4,000 feet above sea level.

All coffee is liquored – that is, tasted – before it is bought. The normal practice is that roasters buy the beans to roast themselves rather than buying it ready-roasted in the country of production. The main reason for this is that, once it has been roasted, the shelf-life of coffee is very short. A second reason is that most European and American retailers prefer to buy direct from a local roaster so that they have greater control over the quality.

Coffee warehouse, Colombia.

EXPORTING THE BEANS

Between 5 and 6 million tons of green coffee are produced each year. Most of this will begin the journey from the plantations on which it was grown on a pack animal, but then its journey to the tables of the world will be by road, river, rail and, today, air.

As we have seen, until it is ready to be sold and exported, the beans are kept and transported in their parchment shells. Although this increases the bulk and therefore the costs of storage and transportation, the parchment does protect the beans. Almost all green beans are packed in coarse fiber bags made of jute or sisal, most of which hold 130 pounds. In Hawaii, bags holding 100 pounds are common; in Colombia 150-pound bags are preferred; and in Puerto Rico 200-pound bags are sometimes used.

The bags are shipped in containers that hold around 250 standard bags or sometimes on wooden pallets, and it has been estimated that some 2,250 ships are involved in moving coffee around the world. Pests and humidity can cause serious problems during transit. When it arrives at its destination, the coffee is then either sent on to another warehouse or sent direct to the roaster.

Loading coffee bags on ship, Brazil.

32

TASTING COFFEE

Different coffees come from all around the world and are prepared in a variety of ways, offering the drinker a huge variety of flavors and styles, ranging from light to full bodied, and from very acidic to lightly acidic. The sheer quantity of varieties can be rather overwhelming or confusing for a newcomer to gourmet and specialty coffees. However, just as there is a fairly well-defined and widely understood system for appraising wines, so there is a similar system for coffee.

A professional taster will have a selection of arcane equipment, including a large number of white cups or glasses (most of which will be chipped), together with hundreds of sample boxes, trays (one for roasted coffee and one for green coffee), scales for measuring, a small grinder, possibly even a small roaster, a spittoon, tasting spoons, and in the best-equipped and most up-to-date establishments, equipment for measuring the moisture content.

The appearance of beans varies slightly, although to the trained eye, significantly. Some writers, for example, think that washed arabica beans look more "elegant" than robusta beans. In terms of flavor, the coffee from different areas can be loosely classified. Coffee from South America has a bright acid and clean flavor; some East African, Yemeni, and Ethiopian coffees taste winy; arabicas from Indonesia are more heavy-bodied; while Indian coffees are less acid, but can be equally full-bodied.

When a coffee is being appraised, the taster has 10 criteria to consider:

- Type – robusta, washed, arabica
- Taste – strictly soft, harsh
- Body – lacking, too heavy
- Acidity – some, too much at the top
- Age – old to fresh
- Defects – sour, grassy, musty
- Cup – roast, watery, burned, old
- Overall assessment – neutral, spicy, hard
- Aroma – weak to strong
- Fullness – slight to considerable

To become a good coffee liquorer, as a taster is called, takes many years' experience, which is usually gained on the job. Tasting coffee is similar to tasting tea or wine, although it is agreed that wine is easier to taste because it persists on the palate for longer.

The coffee taster first assesses the green beans, noting their appearance and aroma. Next, he smells a freshly ground

Coffee tasting at Jacobs Co., Germany.

sample. After the coffee has infused in water, the taster noses the brew. After 3 minutes, the brew is lightly stirred and smelled again. The resulting foam is removed and the tasting proper begins. The taster takes a spoonful of coffee into his or her mouth and "chews" it around before spitting it out. The procedure is repeated with all the samples, and notes are made as each brew is sampled. Many tasters use a 1–5 or even a 1–10 scale, although others use more individual methods.

Do not be deterred from attempting your own coffee tasting. You will be pleasantly surprised at how quickly you learn to differentiate between different varieties in order to recognize your favorites. You will also be able to ask for interesting and rewarding blends, and in no time you will be creating your own blends. Who knows, you may find that a 70:30 blend of Tanzania Chagga AA and Monsoon Malabar A is your idea of heaven!

The first step, as in wine tasting, is to acquire the correct vocabulary and to gain experience in using it. There is no substitute for drinking different kinds of coffee as often as possible. This will give you an opportunity to find out which kinds are available and which kinds you like – or do not. Everyone has different palates and preferences – some people will find Harrar Longberry excessively winy or will come to the conclusion that Costa Rican coffee is all shine and no substance.

───── COFFEE TASTERS' VOCABULARY ─────

PROFESSIONAL TASTERS USE a variety of scales and notes to describe and assess the brews they taste. Here are just a few of the ways they describe the various aspects they are looking for in each cup:

- Aroma: animal-like, ashy, burned/smoky, chemical/medical, chocolaty, caramel/malty, earthy, floral, fruity, grainy/green/herbal, nutty, rancid/rotten, rubber-like, spicy, tobacco-like, winy, woody
- Taste: acid, bitter, salty, sour, sweet
- Mouth-feel: balance of flavors, astringent, body

Robusta is often mustier and has a more burned flavor, while arabica is more citrus with higher acidity.

TASTING COFFEES AT HOME

Invite two friends to taste three different coffees. For your first tasting, do not look for fine differences, but think about identifying the main characteristics of, say, a South American and an Asian coffee. For example, Ethiopian coffee is high in acidity and low in body, while a Sumatran coffee will have a low acidity and be full-bodied.

You will need three sets of three cups – white, medium-sized ones are best – and a spittoon.

Grind a tablespoon of beans for each taster and put the powder in the bottom of a cup. Professional tasters measure the amount very precisely: some use scales to measure out ⅓ ounce, but others prefer ½ ounce. Write the name of the coffee on a piece of paper and place it under the cup. After grinding one type of bean, shake or brush away as much as possible of the detritus before you grind the next. Professionals will even grind a small amount of the next beans between batches to make sure that none of the previous type is left. You should grind enough beans to allow for a small amount of ground coffee to be presented in a saucer or dish near the tasting sample.

Incidentally, the grinder must be a good one and be able to produce a consistent grind. Slasher or wing grinders are not ideal, and you are looking for a grinding that will provide grounds of 00.008–0.002 inch with 7–8 percent powder. You are looking for powder that is suitable for a drip machine because this will release the aroma over the optimum period. Too fine, and the aroma will be released too soon; too coarse, and insufficient aroma will be released.

The amount of water is also precisely measured because too much will make the coffee watery, while too little will make it harsh. Draw the water freshly from a cold faucet, allowing it to run for a few seconds before you fill a kettle or pot. Turn off the water just before it boils and pour it onto the ground beans. If you have ⅓ ounce of coffee in an average-sized cup, you need to fill the cup to just below the rim. Make sure that the water is equally hot for each cup, bringing it back to near boiling point for each one if necessary. If you live in an area that has very hard water, you may need to boil it first to remove some of the chalk, which can affect the flavor. Some tasters prefer to make coffee in a pot and pour it into the tasting cups, but most pour the water directly onto the ground coffee in individual cups.

Although the technical word for tasting coffee is "cupping," many tasters say that clear glasses are better. These make it possible to inspect the brew more closely. If you decide to use glasses, choose ones that are wider at the top than wine glasses (which should be wider in the center than at the top). The wider glasses make it possible to appreciate the aroma.

The taster first "noses" the fresh ground coffee, then the cup or glass into which the water has been poured. At this stage the brew is not stirred. After 2–3 minutes, nose the coffee again, using a silver-plated spoon (a soup spoon is ideal) to break the crust that will have formed on the surface. This will give you your first impression of the coffee.

Take a couple of sniffs. Remember that our olfactory sense diminishes after only 2–4 seconds' exposure to a smell, which is our body's way of dealing with all the new smells it picks up throughout the day. If it did not and the old smells were retained in our consciousness, they would mingle with the new. Some tasters try nosing with alternate nostrils, but often a few seconds' break is enough to revive your sense of smell. Write down your first impressions. Was the coffee earthy, ashy, floral – or something else altogether? When you are tasting, try to be precise and to use the same kinds of words that other tasters use.

── TASTING COFFEE AT HOME ──

1 Assemble green beans, grinds, and spoon as shown.

2 Pour near-boiling water onto grinds.

3 "Nose" coffee, then break crust of grind that has formed.

4 Nose coffee again, then "suck" a spoonful into your mouth.

——— BLIND TASTING ———

AFTER A BLIND tasting of six different coffees (from Brazil, Cameroon, Colombia, Costa Rica, Ivory Coast, and Kenya) among a group of French consumers, the International Coffee Organization found that:

- Colombian coffee was rated as having the strongest aroma; it was rated significantly higher than Costa Rican, Cameroonian, Brazilian, and Kenyan. Only coffee from the Ivory Coast was higher for some tasters.

- Acidity was a difficult characteristic for the tasters to assess. Costa Rican and Colombian coffees were found to have the most acidity. Very dark-roast coffees tend to lose almost all their acidity, unlike light-roast coffees, which develop high acidity.

- Kenyan coffee was perceived to be significantly less bitter than Colombian, Costa Rican, and Brazilian coffees, although they were dark roasted and somewhat bitter, but not less bitter than the two robusta coffees. (A dark roast increases bitterness more in arabica than in robusta coffee, but Kenyan beans are the exception that proves this general rule.)

- A fruity flavor, which might be expected to disappear with a very dark roast, was still identified by the tasters, and Kenyan coffee was perceived as being markedly more fruity than the two robustas, but not significantly more fruity than the Brazilian, Colombian, and Costa Rican coffees.

- When the tasters were asked to identify burned flavors, the results were similar to the tasting for bitterness. The participants could be divided into two groups – those who could distinguish the burned characteristics and those who could not. Both Costa Rican and Colombian coffees were, however, perceived as having a noticeably greater degree of burned aroma/flavor than the Kenyan coffee.

- When it came to assessing body, Costa Rican coffee was found to be the most full-bodied, and the difference was most notable when the coffee was compared with the coffees from Kenya, Brazil, Ivory Coast, and Cameroon, although it was less marked when compared with Colombian coffee.

- On average, all the coffees were regarded as having an after-taste of medium intensity, with the Costa Rican coffee scoring significantly higher than all three of the coffees from Africa.

In general, the tasters expressed a preference for Kenyan coffee over those from Brazil, Colombia, and Ivory Coast, with the other two coffees coming second after the Kenyan coffee. .

This tasting shows that, at least among this group of French consumers, the preferred coffee was the one that had the lowest intensities of aroma and bitterness, the lowest intensity of burned and full-bodied characteristics and a high degree of fruitiness. Colombian coffee, which has the opposite characteristics to Kenyan coffee, was significantly less liked than the African bean, and although the coffee from Cameroon was very close to the Kenyan coffee, it was perceived as being more bitter and definitely less fruity.

Repeat this exercise with all the coffees you are tasting – and don't forget to rinse your spoon in clean water between coffees.

Next, gently stir the brew and take up a spoonful. Suck this into your mouth, slurping rather than drinking. You may think that this looks (and sounds) inelegant, and it does. But you are all doing it, so there is no need to stand on ceremony or to be shy. "Chew" the coffee around your mouth to get some idea of the acidity and body. The sense of body is an important one – is the coffee full-bodied or not? Acidity is more difficult to define, but you will feel it on the edge of your tongue. Spit out the coffee and write down your impressions.

Views differ on the second tasting. Many people feel that tea and coffee are harder to taste than wine because the alcohol in wine encourages persistence on the palate and helps to create an identity. Some tasters find it difficult to measure the range of variables in tea and coffee with one or even two tastings. You might, therefore, want to try all the coffees being tasted, "chewing" them to measure the body and acidity, and then to taste them again, but this time more aggressively. This time you are looking for individual characteristics and flavors – is it sweet or salty, is there a flavor of charcoal or is it musty? To taste properly, you must "slurp" as hard as you can, drawing the coffee into the back of the mouth and spraying the soft palate. You will probably be making a lot of noise and quite a mess, but you are hopefully also having some fun, too. Remember to make a note of your impressions.

After 15 minutes, by which time the brews will have cooled, taste them again.

WITH OR WITHOUT MILK?

MILK, THAT WELL-KNOWN companion of coffee, should not be taken with coffee that is being seriously tasted. It will affect the flavor. At other times, a light-bodied coffee should always be drunk black, although a heavy-bodied one will survive the addition of milk. When you are tasting, however, never add milk.

ROASTING COFFEE

When it is done well, roasting coffee beans is an art. The process creates flavor and aroma, and without it none of the flavor of coffee is apparent in the cup. Green beans are relatively stable and, if stored correctly, will last for years.

During roasting, the heat causes a series of chemical reactions to take place. Starches are converted into sugars, some kinds of acids are created, and others are broken down. The basic cellular structure of the bean eventually melts, causing the bean to "pop" just like popcorn. Proteins are broken down into peptides, and these emerge through the surface of the bean in the form of oils. Moisture and carbon dioxide are burned off and, for a darker roast, pure carbon will be created.

The aromatic oils are really at the heart of roasting. They are called coffee essence, coffee oil, or more accurately, caffeol.

The aromatic oils are volatile – that is, they are the elements that carry the flavors and aromas – and they are water-soluble, which means that those flavors and aromas can be enjoyed in the cup. The great enemies of roasted beans are oxygen and, to a lesser extent, light, for as soon as beans are roasted, they begin to lose the flavors that have been brought to the surface by roasting. The oils that have been precipitated to the surface are oxidized, and in no time at all, they produce a sooty, rancid flavor.

Coffee roasting plant in the U.S.

The roaster himself can cause untold damage. If the beans have not been roasted either to the necessary temperature or for long enough, the oils will not have been brought out to the surface, and the flavor will be bready. If the roasting is done at too high a temperature or for too long, the beans will taste thin and burned. Burned coffee is very unpleasant.

Most roasters are gas-fired. They work at temperatures of around 550°F, and for the first 5 minutes or so the high temperature burns off any free moisture. Thereafter, the residual moisture is forced from the beans (this causes the cracking or popping sound). Next, when the beans reach a temperature of about 400°F, they start to turn a darker brown, and it is at this point that the oils start to emerge. This process is called pyrolysis. From this point, the person who is roasting has to begin to make crucial decisions, for if the beans are left for too long, they will be ruined.

Larger machines, of the kind that are found in commercial roasters, move the beans along a screw inside the drum, and when they reach the end of the screw, they are done. Such expensive machines are viable only when large quantities of beans are being roasted. A local specialty roaster will probably use what is known as a "batch" roaster, which is basically a drum, rotating horizontally, with a fire beneath and a fan to draw away the smoke and fumes.

A smaller retailer will probably use a 25-pound machine, while a serious amateur or a retailer who is very concerned about freshness might prefer one of the tabletop roasters that are now becoming available.

Some typical roasts (FROM LEFT): unroasted, medium roast, medium to full roast, high roast, Continental roast, and French roast.

—————— ROASTER'S VOCABULARY ——————

FOLLOWING ARE JUST some of the words used to describe the same roast. Ask your coffee merchant to explain so you can describe precisely what you want.

- Light roasts: half city, cinnamon, New England, light
- Medium: full city, American, medium/high, breakfast, regular, brown
- Medium/high to dark: light French, Viennese, city, full city
- Dark/high roast: continental, New Orleans, European, French, after dinner, Italian
- Very dark roast: dark French, heavy

It is important that the beans are kept moving during the roasting process, not only to make sure that the batch roasts evenly, but also to stop them from burning, which could cause them to catch fire.

When the beans are taken from the roaster, they are cooled, preferably by air, but sometimes in water. The more quickly and completely the cooling is done, the better, because roasted beans will continue to cook as they cool down.

The only universal terminology among coffee roasters are the words "low," "medium," and "high," or sometimes, "light," "medium," and "dark," and these words mean different things to different people. In the U.S. the vocabulary is wider, with expressions such as "full city roast," which means usually that the beans have been taken to the stage just before they would become "high," "dark," or "European."

There is no reason why you cannot mix a light- with a dark-roast bean if that is what you want. However, you should bear in mind that some roasts are not appropriate for some coffees, just as some coffees are more appropriate for different times of day.

It would, for example, be a waste to high-roast an Ethiopian bean because you would lose the individual character of the coffee. It would also be a shame to dark-roast Yauco Selecto or Kona beans, because you would lose the classic flavor you bought them for. Other quality gourmet beans will, on the other hand, gain something new and interesting when they are dark-roasted. Mexican beans, for example, become interestingly sweet when they are dark-roasted.

Some coffees, such as Guatemalan Antigua, will retain their acidity and fruit when they are high-roasted. Other coffees are more difficult. Sumatran coffees, for instance, usually have a very full body but low to medium acidity, and at a higher roast they do lose their acidity, but tend to acquire a rather syrupy body.

In general, however, the darker the roast, the lower the eventual quality, and darker roasts mean that less of the true character of the bean will be apparent.

Freshly roasted beans in the cooling pan.

ROASTING BEANS AT HOME

The most difficult coffee-related activity is to roast your own beans at home. However, the freshness of the roasted coffee is the first essential when it comes to brewing quality coffee, and we have all bought stale coffee from a roaster, even if only once. There is absolutely nothing to compare with the taste of beans you have roasted, then ground and made into coffee in your own kitchen. So, it is worth the effort.

The easy way is to roast the beans in the oven. This has the benefit of allowing you to control the temperature so that your home is not completely taken over by the smell of roasting coffee. Preheat your oven to 450°F. Remember that air must be allowed to move under and among the beans, so they must not be spread too thickly. Leave the beans in the oven for about 10 minutes and watch for the color change. Listen for the sounds of the beans cracking, and keep checking the color. When the beans are just a little lighter than you want, take them out of the oven and allow them to cool. The beans will continue to cook internally for another 2–4 minutes.

You can also buy stove-top home roasters, but the best kind are the traditional roaster pan or popcorn-popper types. These have a handle that drives two vertical plates inside the body. The plates rotate the beans as they roast. You might be able to find one in a secondhand store or in a good kitchen store. You will also find an oven thermometer invaluable.

When the beans are ready, take them from the roaster, place in a flameproof bowl, and put it near a window or even outdoors.

Pour green beans into stove-top roaster.

Check temperature during roasting.

GRINDING COFFEE

Whenever coffee is processed, its effective life, in terms of flavor, is shortened. Green beans, as we have noted, can last for years, but after roasting there is only a week of full flavor and, at best, two weeks of half-flavor. After grinding, the coffee's life is reduced to a few days at the most.

In any good coffee store, when you choose the original or blend of beans you want, you will probably be asked if you need the beans to be ground. If you do want them ground, make sure that you specify the method you will be using to brew the coffee, because this will affect the grind. The objective, of course, is to get the most flavor from the beans, and this is done by infusing the ground beans in hot water. Generally, the faster the infusion, the finer the grind.

The basic categories of grind are "coarse," "medium," and "fine." The finer grinds do not need to remain in contact with water for as long as the coarser grinds. The coarsest grind, therefore, is used in the classic pot method. The plunger/cafetiere and drip/filter methods require coarser grinds than espresso, which needs the least amount of time, and the perfect espresso grind is finer than sand. The ideal grind for a pot might be described as painful to walk on barefoot.

The finer/faster rule should only be used as a guide. If, for example, you tried using an espresso grind in your filter machine, you find that the water took longer to filter through and the flavor would not be improved. If you want to make a stronger or weaker brew, it is much better simply to increase or reduce the proportion of ground coffee to water rather than to vary the grind.

GRINDING AT HOME

It cannot be said too often that the best thing of all is to roast, grind, and brew coffee on the spot. This is a counsel of perfection for most people, but it does guarantee a good cup of coffee. However, even if we had all the equipment, most of us will have to be content with grinding beans just before we prepare the brew. The difference between freshly ground coffee beans and beans that were ground only a few days before is huge.

TYPES OF GRINDS

fine espresso grind

fine grind

medium grind

medium coarse grind

coarse grind

pulverized

Grinding your own beans is easy to do. There are lots of different grinders on the market; they are not too frightening to buy, and they take up little room in the kitchen.

The oldest way to reduce beans to a brewable form is by mortar and pestle. If you must use this, you must, but it is not quick and the results are not consistent, producing grounds that are suitable only for longer infusion methods or for Turkish coffee.

The second oldest method is probably the millstone – and it is possibly the best. The grinder originated in the Middle East and is a hand-held cylinder, containing the equivalent of two millstones in the form of two corrugated steel disks, which crush the beans.

Next comes the wooden box grinder. You put the beans in the top and, after grinding, pull them out in the little drawer at the bottom. It is worth paying extra to get the best possible quality. Not only will it last for years, but the cheaper versions just do not produce a fine, consistent grind.

The fourth main type is the wall-mounted or table-fitted type of grinder or mincer. These are good, solid metal objects, made by, among other companies, Spong.

Basic grinder consisting of a box with a drawer to catch the coffee.

*Early 20th-century table-fitted grinder
made from solid metal.*

The next group consists of electric, motor-driven machines, which can either have blades or two crushing burr plates. The very top of the range is the Gaggia MDF which, at time of writing, retails for around $200. The MDF has 36 different grind settings, and the great advantage of this kind of grinder is that you can get the exact quantity with just the degree of fine or coarse or medium grind that you want. If you have one of the hand-held grinders, you need to measure out the precise number of beans and then grind for varying lengths of time to get the kind of grind you require. If you drink espresso, you will need one of these more expensive machines, because a hand-held grinder simply will not produce the consistently fine grind that is essential.

A coarse grind will require 7–10 seconds, a medium grind will take 10–13 seconds, and a fine grind (although not for espresso) will take 15–20 seconds.

BLADES VS BURRS

There can be no doubt that burrs give a much better grind than a blade. A blade does not so much mill or grind the beans; it slashes them, first to ribbons and then to irregular pieces. Around the edge will be a fine powder, while there will be chunks of bean at the center.

However, freshly slashed beans still have much more flavor than long-stored ground coffee, and the blade grinders do have one advantage over the burr grinders – they are much cheaper. A Bosch hand-held grinder retails for around one-fifth of the price of the Gaggia MDF.

Nevertheless, if you have the opportunity to compare the flavors resulting from the two grinding methods, you may be surprised at the extra edge of quality that results from the even grind produced by burrs.

Ideally, keep your hand-held blade grinder for vacations, second homes, extensive traveling, and so on. If you must use one, do not hold your finger on the button for a long time. Grind in bursts of 2–5 seconds, which prevents the beans from heating up too much, and give it a gentle shake or tap it on the table to jiggle the contents around between bursts.

Gaggia MDF – one of the best grinders available.

MAKING COFFEE

Perhaps one of the reasons that the drinking and enjoyment of coffee has spread so widely around the world is that it lends itself so well to so many different ways of preparation and satisfies so many different palates. Nevertheless, the basic principle is universal and common to all methods of making coffee: the ground beans are soaked in hot water to extract a liquor with flavor and aroma.

Although the coffee bean came to us from Arabia, the Arabian way of making coffee did not spread, and even though there are now dozens of ways to make coffee, there is still a fundamental difference between all these methods and the traditional Arabian way, in which coffee is boiled three times. Boiling coffee is bad, because it boils off the caffeol flavors and aromas, and it exaggerates the bitter-tasting elements in the infusion. To overcome this, Arabs added cardamom to their coffee. We tend to look to machinery and technology.

There is no one "best" method of making coffee. The "best" method is the one that suits you, and you have to consider your own convenience and preferences and the time the different methods take. There is also, of course, the indefinable element of the ritual involved in making coffee. As a break during a busy day or after a stressful time in the office, it can be fun to take the time to make a really good cup of coffee – just for yourself.

Coffee set by Pirandelli.

A PERFECT CUP OF COFFEE

THERE ARE SEVEN simple rules to observe if you want to make a good cup of coffee every time:

- Use freshly roasted beans, preferably roasted no more than a week ago, ideally half an hour ago
- Store the beans in an airtight container
- Grind the beans immediately before brewing
- Use fresh, cold water, drawn from a faucet that has been allowed to run for a few seconds. Bring the water to a boil, but do not overboil, and do not pour boiling water on the coffee
- Use the method you prefer – plunger, drip, or whatever – and allow the coffee long enough to brew
- Drink the freshly brewed coffee as soon as possible
- Remember to warm your cup or mug before you pour in the coffee

---

TURKISH COFFEE

The coffee that we call Turkish is, perhaps, made in the same way as the earliest coffee drinkers used to brew their beans. Ground coffee, sugar, and water are put, in that order, into a small brass jug with a long handle, called an ibriq. You should use 2 level teaspoons of coffee for each cup and add 1 teaspoon of sugar for each teaspoon of coffee. When the brew has boiled, take it off the heat. As it boils, the liquid rises up the neck of the ibriq, so make sure that you do not fill it to the brim. The brew is brought to a boil three times in all before being served. Traditionally, cardamom is added to this kind of coffee. You can buy and grind your own (do not use your coffee grinder for the cardamom seeds), and you will need one seed for each cup.

It has to be said that this is not a good way to treat good coffee, but it is an interesting drink and has an individual taste.

Coffee pot (ibriq) *for brewing Turkish-style coffee.*

PERCOLATOR

The percolator was invented in 1827 in France and became very popular in the United States. It does produce a wonderful aroma in the home and a satisfying sound as the water gurgles through and around the system. That said, however, percolators boil coffee and produce a bitter-tasting brew.

American Universal percolator from the 1880s.

CONA VACUUM

The vacuum method of making coffee was devised in 1840 by Robert Napier, a Scottish marine engineer. It works on the principle of a globe, half-filled with water, being placed over a heat source with dry coffee in a receiver above. When it is stable, the heat source is removed and the coffee enters the globe by means of a syphon between the two. This was later marketed under the Cona brand name.

You may sometimes see these machines in restaurants, and you may even come across one in a secondhand store (although the glass globes are fragile and easily cracked). There is something rather alchemical about the method, and it is an interesting way of making coffee, which can be excellent if you take care not to let the coffee itself boil. They are not convenient for everyday use.

An original Cona balloon, once a popular method of brewing coffee.

THE DRIP METHOD

The drip or filter method, the most popular system in the West today, was invented by a Frenchman, M. de Belloy.

The unit is in two halves. The hot water is poured over coarsely ground coffee, which is held in a paper filter in the upper section. The brew drips down, by gravity, through the filter into the pouring pot below. This takes 6–8 minutes, and the result is a clear drink that contains few grounds.

Electric versions of this method, called filter machines, are able to produce the correct amount of water at the optimum temperature for making the most of the beans before it passes through a permanent or paper filter. One of the advantages of a paper filter is the convenience – you simply throw it away after use. Paper also provides a more comprehensive filtration material than the permanent filters in some machines.

There are several styles, makes, and additional features available, although none of them seems to have much effect on the final cup. The main supplier of the self-pour drip units is Melitta. Of the permanent filters, the best are the "gold"

Krups combination filter/espresso/cappuccino maker.

ones, which allow more sediment elements into the coffee and thereby give it a different texture. These machines require a slightly coarser grind.

The correct hand-drip method is to use cold water and bring it almost to a boil. Warm the pot and pour away the water. Pour some water into the ground coffee to initiate some caffeol activity, then pour in the required amount of water.

The Germans seem to make the best of the filter machines. Krups is top of the line; Braun is the most stylish; and Melitta is the best value. At the lower end of the market are Novelco and Proctor-Silex.

FRENCH PRESS OR CAFETIERE

Known as the French press, the Meloir in the United States, and the cafetiere in Europe, the plunger pot system is an excellent way to make coffee. Many people prefer coffee made this way because it extracts the full flavor from the ground beans while other methods tend to remove some of the taste, and paper filters can even add a taste of their own. The plunger pot is said to have been invented in 1933 by an Italian called Caliman who sold the design and patent to a Swiss national in order to escape from Italy during the war.

The method could not be simpler. Warm the pot, put in the coarsely ground coffee (about ⅙ ounce) for each cup), add the hot water, stir, and allow to steep for 4–5 minutes. Then push down the plunger – a stainless steel mesh – to separate the grounds from the liquid before serving the coffee direct from the press, which looks attractive on the table.

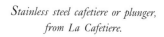

Stainless steel cafetiere or plunger, from La Cafetiere.

This is a convenient method, because the grounds are so easily disposed of, and it is possible to enjoy the full flavor of the coffee. There is also the advantage that you can buy different sizes of pot, so you do not have to use the eight-cup size when you are making your breakfast-time coffee. The only drawback is that if you make a brew for, say, after dinner, it will get cold quickly when it is left standing on the table. You can buy ceramic or even thermos-type presses (although this may be going a bit far), or you could use one of the "tea cozies" that are now coming on the market. Alternatively, make a pot of fresh coffee.

The Danish company Bodum makes the best of the less expensive presses, while the top of the line includes the French-made Meloir and the U.K. La Cafetiere. Alessi also produces an excellent model. The main point to look out for when you are buying a plunger pot is not to try to save money by buying one with a nylon mesh. A stainless steel mesh is much better and will last far longer.

ESPRESSO, MOCHA, AND NAPOLITANA

These three words – espresso, mocha, and napolitana – all describe those neat little stove-top makers of very dark coffee that seem to exist in every Italian kitchen. They have two chambers, and the water, which is in the lower one, is forced through the coffee and into the top chamber, from where it is poured. This method has few of the benefits of the plunger pot or filter method, although the little pots are undeniably attractive.

Stove-top espresso pot, the most popular known method of making coffee in Italy.

COLD WATER METHOD

This method is useful if you are making coffee that is going to be used in cold drinks, and it is always useful to have some in stock, especially during the summer. Mix ground coffee with about a quart of cold water and leave for 12 hours. Strain the liquid to remove the grounds and keep it in the refrigerator until you are ready to use it. It has a very strong flavor and will need to be added to normal coffee, in the proportion of 1 cup of extract to about 4 cups of normal coffee. The extract will keep for a while, and many people find it easier to digest than regular coffee because the process extracts few oils and hardly any acidity.

NEAPOLITAN FLIP-TOP

These reversible drip pots have two chambers. The water in the lower one is brought to a boil, and then the pot is turned over so that the water drips through into the coffee chamber before serving. Lovers of fine coffee should note the word "boil."

OPEN POT OR JUG

This, the most basic of methods, is, some believe, still the best way to make coffee. You will need very coarse grounds, which are placed in the bottom of the pot. Pour on the water, stir, allow to steep, and pour, using a strainer to remove any grounds. Tradition says that an eggshell placed in the pot will absorb some of the sediment.

Danish Shelton stainless steel coffee pot by Arne Jacobsen, 1970s.

ESPRESSO AND CAPPUCCINO

Whatever else is uncertain about coffee – its origins, the most flavorful beans, the best way of brewing – you can be sure of one thing: whenever two or more serious coffee drinkers get together, they will discuss the finer points of making espresso and cappuccino.

Espresso is a brewing process by which the classic, dark-roasted cup of black coffee – full-bodied but aromatic – is made, and it is possibly the most difficult and potentially the most expensive way to make coffee. The word *espresso* derives from the Italian verb meaning "to put under pressure," and that is exactly how the coffee is made. Boiling water and steam are forced through very finely ground coffee – preferably one without too much acidity, so Kenyan is not ideal – to produce a unique style of coffee with bite and great persistence on the palate. It is not just the rich, sweet flavor that makes espresso such a wonderful drink – when it is good, it has an indefinable tang, a quality that fills the palate.

Authentic espresso accounts for only 10 percent of Italian coffee, although it is, literally, the basis of the other 90 percent, which is cappuccino – espresso with a milky froth on top. Ideally, cappuccino is one-third espresso, one-third milk, and one-third froth. The fact that the major coffee suppliers are now offering instant cappuccino is an indication of consumers' acceptance of and desire for espresso and cappuccino.

LEFT The latest, and smallest, espresso/cappuccino maker.

RIGHT Carmencita coffee pot by Lavazza.

La Pavoni, commercial espresso/cappuccino maker, 1930s.

Indifferent cappuccino is universally available, which is perhaps an indication that it is easier to make a cup that tastes pleasant than it is to produce good espresso. Really good cappuccino is, however, even more difficult to make than espresso. Every cup must be freshly made by a method that gets the best from the coffee – unlike espresso, a little acidity is desirable in cappuccino, and Kenyan coffee can be used – but the real difficulty lies in preparing the milk, which must not be allowed to boil, or its chemical character will alter and affect the overall flavor. Some people do not like chocolate on top, but it does stop a skin from forming if the milk has been allowed to boil.

There are two main types of espresso machines available: piston-operated machines and electric machines.

Piston-operated machines have a spring-loaded system that forces the water through the coffee. These piston-handled machines look wonderful, and in the hands of a skilled *barista*, they produce excellent coffee. They are not ideal for less-experienced operators, however, and more and more people are turning to the fully automated machines that make it possible simply to turn a switch and wait until the cup is one-third or three-quarters full before switching it off. These days the only skill seems to lie in getting the milk for cappuccino to froth, which takes time and practice. The electric espresso machine is easier to operate and more practical. If you are thinking of purchasing a machine, it is no good trying to economize. The cheaper models that are available do not generate enough steam and pressure to make real espresso.

Gaggia piston-operated espresso maker, 1930s.

La Pavoni Professional copper and brass espresso maker.

Espresso Cappuccino Mark 2 by La Pavoni with a funnel that takes milk directly from the carton and delivers it perfectly into the cup.

Krups makes a good range of machines, as do Gaggia, Olympia, Victoria Arduino, and Faema Elespren. Among the most impressive-looking espresso machines are those made by La Pavoni. The company's line includes models that are used in cafés and restaurants, but it also has smaller models. The company claims that its Espresso-Cappuccino model will guarantee to produce a perfect *crema* no matter what blend or grind of coffee is used. Lavazza also produces a selection of machines for espresso and cappuccino.

Many of these manufacturers produce complete sets of grinder and espresso and cappuccino machines. They are not cheap, but think how much you spend every morning if you stop and have a couple of espressos in a café on your way to work.

MAKING ESPRESSO

Making good espresso at home is one of life's little challenges. It is worth remembering that the more you are prepared to spend on a machine, the better the coffee will be. However, making good espresso should be regarded as a hobby – not as a lifetime's search for perfection.

Various accoutrements needed to make espresso and cappuccino.

*A tamper is used to pack down the
ground coffee in the filter basket.*

*The best coffee comes out first
— black, then the crema.*

*Switch off before the coffee
becomes bitter and watery.*

First, select the coffee. Almost all the coffee sold in specialty stores for espresso comes from arabica beans, but there is no such thing as a specific espresso bean or roast. Because the process of making espresso tends to intensify the characteristics of whatever bean you select, you will probably want to use a blend. Peet's in the U.S. uses four types of bean in its espresso blend, but you might want to begin with a combination of an aromatic and fairly acidic Central American bean and a rich, full-bodied Indonesian bean.

Next, grind your beans. They should be fine, but not pulverized as they would be for, say, Turkish coffee. If you have a Gaggia MDF, use the 3 or 4 setting. The grind is crucial: if it is too coarse, the coffee will gush out thin and watery, but if it is too fine, the coffee will drip too slowly and be bitter. You will need 1½–2 level tablespoons to a cup.

Apart from grind, another common problem is the tamping down of the ground beans into the machine. They must not be so loose that the water gushes straight through, but they must not be tamped so tightly that nothing can get through. In a good machine, you will need to tamp the grounds down in the *gruppa* firmly and quite vigorously. At first, you may find it helpful to examine a just-used *gruppa* to check that you are tamping correctly.

When the coffee begins to come out from the nozzles under the *gruppa*, remember that the best comes first – the black, then the caramel-colored *crema* – switch off now, because if you leave the machine on too long the coffee will be bitter and watery.

The vital indication of whether a cup of espresso is a good one is the presence of *crema*. As the coffee is discharged into the cup, it should be covered with a caramel-colored layer, the *crema*, which is created by the oils in the coffee mixing water and air during the extraction process. The *crema* should be evenly colored and as much as ¼ inch thick. As you drink, it should coat the side of the cup like syrup. A dark-brown *crema* with a white dot or black hole in the middle is a sign that the espresso has been over-extracted and will taste harsh and bitter. A light-colored *crema*, on the other hand, indicates an under-extracted espresso that will taste weak.

Good, evenly colored crema.

Over-extracted espresso produces thin crema.

Light tamping can cause light crema.

The kind of coffee you use is a matter of personal preference. Some research has shown that people who like espresso and who buy espresso machines are not the same people who like original and gourmet coffees. Traditionally, the character of espresso demands a high-roast bean, although a medium-roast coffee will do just as well. Until you get used to your machine, try richer, sweeter, dark-roast beans for espresso and keep the light to medium beans for your French press.

By the way, did you know that four 1-ounce shots of espresso have about the same caffeine content as one mug of regular-brewed coffee.

——— MAKING CAPPUCCINO ———

Place steam jet just under surface of milk.

Gently place froth on coffee using a spoon.

A sprinkle of chocolate stops boiling milk from forming a skin, and it tastes good.

MAKING CAPPUCCINO

Once the fresh coffee is in the cup, begin to prepare the milk. You should always try to use 2-percent homogenized, because full-fat milk will mask the flavor of the coffee; and although some cafés use milk that is warm or at least at room temperature because it does not take as long to foam as cold milk, use cold milk if you can. Not only does cold milk foam better, the foam lasts longer and tastes fresher. As long as you are not making cappuccino for 10, use cold milk.

Put the milk in a pitcher and immerse the steam valve so that the nozzle is just under the surface of the milk. If it is too high, you will spray the room with milk; if it is too low, you will not get many bubbles. You should hear a hissing noise, rather than a rumble, which will indicate that the nozzle is too deep. Do not use full power, but do not be too timid. You do not want the milk to boil, but you do want to warm it through. The ideal is a mass of small bubbles, which are more stable than bigger ones: any large bubbles should be knocked off or allowed to burst.

THE CUPS

You may have a wonderful, state-of-the-art espresso machine, and you may be using perfectly ground, freshly roasted beans – but when it comes out of the machine, the coffee is not right. The *crema* does not have that smooth, creamy look. The problem could be that the cup was cold. Try storing the cups upside down on top of the machine so that they are warm before you add the coffee. By the way, for purists, only bone china cups are an acceptable vessel from which to drink coffee.

Bone china cups or mugs, warmed,
are best for drinking coffee.

——— ESPRESSO MENU ———

- **Espresso ristretto** is made by "cutting off" the machine – that is, by switching it off sooner than in regular espresso so that the coffee is denser and more aromatic.
- **Doppio** "double" gives you twice the amount.
- **Americano** is a normally brewed espresso that has been thinned by hot water.
- **Caffé latte** is made by adding milk, steamed to 150–170ºF, to a freshly drawn shot of espresso. Sometimes served in a tall glass, it is finished with a quarter inch of foamed milk and, if liked, a generous sprinkle of chocolate or cinnamon.
- **Espresso macchiato** is a basic espresso that is "marked" with just a little milk.
- **Latte macchiato** is, basically, a glass of hot milk with a little espresso dribbled into it.
- **Espresso romano** is espresso with a twist of lemon peel.
- **Con panna** is espresso with a spoonful of cold whipped cream.
- **Caffé Mocha** is one-third espresso, one-third hot chocolate, and one-third steamed milk, added to the cup in that order. However, you may see caffé mocha made with a generous helping of mocha syrup – enough to coat the bottom of the cup – followed with a shot of espresso and added steamed milk. If you're feeling indulgent, crown it with a scoop of whipped cream and lightly sprinkle with ground sweet cocoa.

Café latte.

BUYING COFFEE

Coffee began as an "original" or "gourmet" coffee, and it was certainly an "estate" coffee, if only because people consumed the coffee that was grown closest to them. As trade developed, however, blending took over, and today, although the best coffees from a single estate or an original coffee from a specific country can be drunk "straight" (or unblended), coffee is essentially a blended drink – just as champagne and some wines are. Indeed, some people would argue that the best coffee is achieved by blending the best character- istics from a range of different coffees – bright acidity from one, a floral aroma from another, full-bodied richness from a third – to make, in Florence Fabricant's words, "a beverage that is good to the last drop."

There have been times when blending has been something of an art form – Mocha Mysore is a popular blend of two quite different types of coffee, in which the soft richness of Mysore combines with the gamey flavor of Mocha – but on the whole it is done for commercial reasons. Robusta is blended with arabica chiefly to reduce the price of arabica, and there can be no doubt that almost all blends are created to produce greater profit than if the individual coffees were sold separately.

The watchword in blending must be consistency. All commercial blenders are looking for continuity of flavor, and some are excellent – for example, Finland's Paulig, Sweden's Gevalia, Zeogas, and Avid Norquist, and Douwe Egberts from the Netherlands, are all good coffees with a lot of character.

An ideal introduction for a new coffee drinker might be a breakfast blend, which will be available from a good roaster. This is often made from a blend of African coffees for drinking with milk, or it might be a blend of two medium roasts of Kenyan and Colombian coffees to give a sharp,

Some of the large choice of coffees available from Douwe Egberts.

aromatic flavor to start the day. An after-dinner blend also often comes from the same source, but is darker roasted for extra strength. A very strong but well-balanced after-dinner coffee would be a blend of mature coffee from Indonesia made more racy and elegant by a touch of Kenyan and Costa Rican coffees.

The strongly flavored, very dark-roasted coffee blends have an apparent initial bitterness, but you soon get used to it. The most extreme instance of power in a cup would be a black-roasted continental blend, which, when made as espresso, produces that coffee with the characteristic bitter bite that is popular with southern Italians, although, it has to be admitted, with few others. Espresso blends from northern Italy are more lightly roasted, and they have a delicate defining balance and acidity that is more akin to fine wine.

There is nothing to stop you from creating your own blends, but it is not a good idea to mix opposites such as Ethiopian and Sumatran. The winy quality of the Ethiopian beans will make the straightforward flavor of the Sumatran beans seem muddy. But there is no reason you should not try a good Colombian with, say, a Sumatran, or experiment by adding high-roast beans to a medium roast to bring out the best in both.

When you are faced with a choice of 15 or 20 coffees, how do you make an informed choice? As with wine, it is, of course, a personal matter, but it does pay to take advice from specialist coffee merchants, such as Dallis Bros., of Queens, New York, or H. R. Higgins Ltd. in Duke Street, London.

Here, for example, is what David Higgins advises: "For someone who wants a mild and not too bitter coffee, arabicas like Colombian or Tanzanian Chagga would be a good start, although the Chagga has slightly more acidity. For stronger coffees, much depends on the degree of the roast. Certain coffees, especially mild ones from Brazil and Costa Rica, you can roast very dark and, although they have a powerful taste, they will not become bitter. But if you put in robusta beans, it will be less smooth and you will get a more gutsy flavor. You can produce different flavors and different characters with different blends. A good example is the Chagga–Java–Mocha blend, which combines the deep full body of the Java, the delicate acidity of the Chagga, and the gaminess of the Mocha."

HANDLING AND STORING BEANS

The ideal way to buy and make coffee is to buy small amounts of green beans, roast them yourself, and grind them immediately before you want to make the coffee. However, most of us have to buy ready-roasted beans, perhaps in larger quantities than we can use in just a few days.

When you have to store coffee beans, remember that the main enemy is water. The volatile oils are water soluble – which gives us the flavor in the cup – but damp conditions will taint the oils. Do not store coffee in the refrigerator, because, once it has been opened, moisture will condense on the surface of the container.

GUIDE TO THE ORIGINAL COFFEES
—— OF THE WORLD ——

SOUTH AMERICA

BRAZIL	The dominant force in the market, Brazil produces mainly mild, soft coffees from beans grown close to sea level. The best is Santos, from the Sao Paulo region – it is very smooth with no bitterness.
COLOMBIA	Full-bodied and mellow, with a gentle acidity and slightly nutty flavor. High-quality coffee comes from the beans grown at high altitude.

CENTRAL AMERICA

COSTA RICA	Mild, fragrant coffee with delicate acidity. The Tarrazu region produces richer, more harmonious flavors.
GUATEMALA	Versatile coffee: when it is light-roasted, it is mild and full; when it is dark-roasted, it becomes smoky and powerful.

CARIBBEAN

PUERTO RICO	Increasingly popular coffees with a rich flavor. An up-and-coming source, largely because of U.S. investment.
JAMAICA	Blue Mountain coffee is produced in tiny quantities at 5,000 feet above sea level. Very expensive, but, at their best, very subtle coffees of great finesse.

GUIDE TO THE ORIGINAL COFFEES
———— OF THE WORLD ————

EAST AFRICA

KENYA

The king of East African coffees, noted for its aroma and pleasant sharpness; this is good drunk black or with milk, when it retains its lively character.

TANZANIA

Closer in flavor to the rich, delicate coffees of Central America; less acid than Kenyan coffee. Be on the lookout for Chagga.

WEST AFRICA

CAMEROON & IVORY COAST

Strong, quite bitter robusta coffees, which are often used in espresso blends.

ETHIOPIA

Mocha has a strong, gamy flavor; *Harrar Longberry*, which comes from the Black Mountain of Ethiopia, has gamy, winy flavors with notes of blackcurrant.

INDIA AND INDONESIA

MYSORE

Soft, rich coffee with low acidity and a light, winy taste.

JAVA

A heavy, mellow flavor; the coffee is matured before roasting to give a unique flavor.

SUMATRA

Less intense than Java coffee, this has a touch of delicate acidity.

If you have to store coffee for any length of time, it is better to put it in the freezer, making sure that it is in an air-tight bag. Roast beans that are to be kept for longer than a week should always be kept in the freezer. Do not try to thaw the beans when you need them – they can go straight into the grinder.

The other great enemy of coffee is oxygen, which oxidizes the volatile flavors. This is why it is important to grind the beans immediately before you brew. Once coffee has been ground, much more of its surface is exposed to air, which means that oils begin to evaporate, and the flavor vanishes into thin air.

Do not store coffee near to other strong-smelling or strongly flavored products. Like tea, coffee quickly takes up other scents and flavors. Store your coffee in an air-tight, clean container that is kept only for coffee.

If you buy coffee by mail order, purchase only small amounts at a time. Although you might save money by bulk buying, you will lose value as you lose flavor.

PACKAGING

The fresher the beans, the richer and more flavorful the cup. Coffee suppliers go to great lengths, therefore, to protect the freshly roasted beans from air, heat, light, and moisture, all of which impair the flavor.

Within both Europe and the U.S., the packaging of coffee has become something of a problem in itself. Not only are strict national regulations about the use of recyclable materials coming into force in many countries, but some countries within the European Union impose even tighter limits on the kinds of material that may be used. For example, aluminum, which was once widely used, has now fallen from favor. Combine this with increased consumer awareness of the costs – in both economic and environmental terms – of unnecessary packaging, and it is easy to see why many coffee companies are investing so much time and effort into rethinking their packaging policies.

Until recently, most manufacturers relied on double packaging – that is, the coffee was enclosed in an inner packet which was, in turn, inserted into an outer container, often card. Now many companies are beginning to rely on single vacuum packing.

One-way valve bags help to keep the beans fresher longer than the more traditional paper packaging.

In Finland, Paulig has pioneered the use of a single laminate packing, and the company estimates that by doing away with the outer box, it will save over 1,100 tons of cardboard each year. The laminated packages will also save in terms of transportation costs – a load previously carried by seven trucks will now fit into six trucks – and consumers will be able to reseal the bag with an enclosed adhesive tape to lock in the freshness.

In the U.S., Allegro Coffee uses specially designed one-way valve bags to deliver its roaster-fresh beans. Starbucks uses "flavor-lock," thick-walled bags, into which the beans are packed no more than two hours after roasting. A special valve on each bag allows the carbon dioxide, which is released by the fresh beans, to escape, but prevents oxygen, which robs the beans of flavor, from entering.

Whatever the packaging, remember that, once opened, coffee must be stored in a cool, dry, air-tight container.

FLAVORED COFFEES

At present, U.S. buyers have a choice of more than 100 flavored coffees, and some of these coffees are also being introduced with great success into other countries. The trend for flavored coffees, which are produced by spraying beans (often the cheaper varieties) with carrier oils and covering them with flavoring after roasting, began in the U.S. in the 1970s.

Favorite flavors are chocolate, mocha, amaretto, and double chocolate. Orange liqueur and nut flavors are also available, although serious coffee drinkers will probably draw the line at raspberry-, banana- and cream-flavored beans. New to the West is coffee flavored with cardamom, which has long been added to coffee in the Middle East, and in Mexico cinnamon is a popular and traditional addition.

Smaller stores and serious coffee drinkers have a problem in that they will need a separate grinder for flavored beans, because any residue will affect the taste of the next batch of unflavored beans that is ground. You might find it worthwhile

Popular flavorings for coffee include vanilla, coconut, nutmeg, orange, chocolate, lemon, mint, and cinnamon.

to acquire a smaller, cheaper grinder if you develop a taste for these exotic flavors, or to buy pre-ground flavored coffee.

The three top flavors of essence coffee, which is widely available in France and the U.S., are almond, vanilla, and hazelnut. These sell mostly in summer, when flavored iced coffee can be a refreshing beverage and when regular coffee is drunk less often.

———— MILK ————

THE MOST WIDELY used flavoring in coffee is milk. Traditionally, in countries such as Yemen, Ethiopia, and Turkey, milk is never added to coffee, and it is not, of course, added to espresso.

It is thought that milk was first added to coffee in Grenoble by Sieur Monin in 1685. By the mid-1980s, 57 percent of coffee drinkers in the U.S., and an astonishing 81 percent of German coffee drinkers, took milk in their coffee – these figures are interesting because German coffee is vastly superior to its U.S. equivalent. Perhaps even more surprising is the fact that 27 percent of U.S. drinkers and 43 percent of German drinkers added a sweetener.

The fats in full-cream milk will mask the subtle flavors of coffee, so use half-fat or low-fat milk whenever possible. Heat it carefully, because hot, but not boiled milk can add a delicious silkiness to coffee.

Café au lait.

CAFFEINATED OR DECAF?

Those who claim that "coffee doesn't taste the same without caffeine" are only partly right. Apart from a slightly bitter taste, caffeine itself does not taste of anything very much. The coffee will only taste different if any of the other elements that contribute to a coffee's flavor are removed when the caffeine is taken out.

Green beans that are to be decaffeinated are shipped to Switzerland or Germany from where, after treatment, they are shipped on to the roasting center, which may be anywhere in the world. It is quite possible for a bean grown in Mexico to be shipped to Switzerland, where it is decaffeinated, before being shipped back across the Atlantic to a roaster in San Diego.

The earliest means of decaffeinating coffee was the solvent method, in which the beans were steamed to open them up, soaked in solvent to destroy the caffeine, and then steamed again to remove the traces of solvent. Next, the industry adopted the methylene chloride method, which has the advantage that it does not seem to attract the other flavorings. Because of its association with the depletion of the ozone layer, methylene chloride has been banned from use in Europe beginning in 1995.

The Swiss Water Process, which was patented by Coffex SA in 1979, uses nothing but water and carbon filters. The process, which is expensive, involves soaking the beans in water. This removes the caffeine and the flavors. The caffeine is removed from the water by an activated carbon filter, the beans are dried in a tank and the water, still containing the flavor, is evaporated and reduced to a flavor concentrate, which is sprayed onto the dried beans.

One solution, if you want to cut down on your intake of caffeine but don't want to drink less coffee, is to drink half and half – decaffeinated *and* regular.

Café Hag's decaf option.

COFFEE DRINKING AROUND THE WORLD

Tastes in coffee throughout the world have been changing in recent years and nowhere, as we shall see, as greatly or as quickly as in the U.S. Coffee enthusiasts hope that European countries will follow the U.S. lead toward more estate-grown and original coffees. The traditional European coffee has been a branded blend or a coffee often sold simply as "Guatemalan." As sipping coffees, the branded blends offer consistent, less fragile, and simpler cups than many of the original coffees. However, these coffees will never measure up to a cup of true Yauco Selecto or Kona, and the future for these and other wonderful gourmet coffees looks brighter today than ever before.

Coffee house in Vienna, Austria, where, traditionally you can read, write, or just sit and relax.

FRANCE

France consumes approximately 180,000 tons of coffee a year, and street cafés are so much a part of French life that it would be difficult to imagine a visit to a French city without stopping to enjoy a refreshing cup. On the whole, the French prefer a more dilute brew than is enjoyed in, say, Italy, and it will probably be made of medium roast, coarse-ground beans by the infusion method.

Café Meo is based in Lille, in the north of France, which is a major intersection in road and rail transportation. The company was founded in the 1930s by a Flemish family named Meauxsonne, which was abbreviated to "Meo." It sells only 100 percent arabica coffee, and its selection includes Meo Dégustation (Brazilian, Central American, Ethiopian, and Indian coffees), Meo Gastronomique (Brazilian,

Café Meo's line includes (FROM LEFT): Ethiopian Mocha, Espresso made from pure arabica beans, and the top-of-the-line Prestige.

Colombian, and Mexican coffees) and Prestige (best Santos, Kenyan AA, best Ethiopian, Guatemalan, and Costa Rican). It also offers single coffees from Colombia, Brazil, and Ethiopia. Café Meo also produces private-label and other coffee products, which are available through its chain of 22 stores (15 of which are in the Lille area and the others in Paris). Some Meo stores have in-store roasters and offer, as well as gourmet coffee products, chocolates and fine wines.

Poster by Van Ysendyk, 1925.

FINLAND

Finland is the world's leading coffee consumer, with some 5.7 million drinkers each consuming more than 25 pounds of green coffee annually. Finnish coffee drinkers are very quality conscious, and soluble coffee accounts for only a tiny percent.

Roasters are all locally owned and import 100 percent arabica beans from Colombia (40 percent), Brazil (20 percent), Costa Rica, Guatemala, Nicaragua, and Mexico (20–25 percent), and Kenya (10–15 percent).

The largest share of the retail market, 40 percent, is held by Gustav Paulig, a wholly owned family company. Paulig imported 73,312 tons in the year ending April 1990, of which about 29 percent were Brazilian, 28.6 percent were Colombian, 12.4 percent Costa Rican, 10.8 percent Guatemalan, and 7.2 percent Kenyan. Paulig, which has no soluble or decaffeinated brands, specializes in light-roasted ground beans. The second-largest company is Meira, which has about 31 percent of the market.

Paulig's range of blended coffees: Juhla Mokka, Gustav Paulig, and Presidentti.

GERMANY

In terms of volume, Germany is the world's second-largest consumer (after the U.S.), but in terms of per-capita consumption, it is eighth in the world (which is far higher than the U.S.). Consumption has risen from 13½ pounds to 16¼ pounds per person, and the largest supplier is Colombia, at 130-pound bags, followed by Brazil at 994 bags. The preferred coffee is lightly roasted, coarsely ground, and espresso is at present a small, if growing, sector.

The country's leading coffee producer, Jacobs Kaffeespezialgesellschaft, was founded in Bremen, Germany, in 1885. In 1970 Suchard and Tobler merged to make Interfood, which merged with Jacobs in 1982 to form Jacobs Suchard. Since June 1990, it has been owned by the American multinational General Foods, a subsidiary of Philip Morris, when Klaus J. Jacobs sold his stake in Jacobs Suchard to Kraft. The company, which is today known as Kraft Jacobs Suchard (KJS), is the third-largest food company in Germany (after Nestlé and Unilever).

Café Auslese from Melitta is a good breakfast coffee.

KJS holds about a quarter of the German market for roast and ground coffees, and it also owns many other small European coffee companies, including Gevalia of Sweden, which some writers include in the top three producers of blended ground coffee in the world. Most of KJS's green beans are bought centrally by Taocac, a separate but wholly owned company, based in Zug, Switzerland.

The roasting business of KJS and General Foods is the largest in the world, although much of this is for soluble coffee. In Germany this accounts for 10 percent of total coffee sales (compared with 30 percent in France and Switzerland and a staggering 80 percent in the U.K.).

After KJS, the leading companies in Germany are Tchibo (18 percent), Aldi (15 percent), Eduschio (12 percent), Melitta (6 percent), which is also available in the U.K., Dallmayer (4.5 percent), and Darboven (2.3 percent). The premium blend is Kronig, which is sold in brick-packs, and the second-best seller is Meisterröstung.

BELGIUM

The leading roaster and retailer of coffee in Belgium is Rombouts which is known in other countries too.

Perhaps more interesting, however, are the smaller companies. One of these, Café Knopes, has two stores and sells a selection of both original and blended coffees. Among the original coffees offered are Colombian Supremo, Kenyan AA, Ethiopian Sidamo and Harrar, Guatemalan Maragogype Superior, Hawaiian Kona, Jamaican Blue Mountain, coffee from Papua New Guinea, Indian Monsoon, Yauco Selecto from Puerto Rico, and Venezuelan Tachira.

Café Knopes also sells an unusual product, entitled *Dix Grands Cafés du Monde* ("Ten Great Coffees of the World"). This includes coffees from Brazil, Colombia, Costa Rica, Kenya, Papua New Guinea, Indonesia, Guatemala, Mexico, and Ethiopia. This is an enterprising selection, and it is available in the U.S. through Bergdorf Goodman in New York. Not only would this be a fascinating gift for someone who is inter-ested in good coffee, but it offers an ideal way to introduce converts to specialty coffees to a wide range of flavors.

ITALY

The Italians drink 33 million cups of coffee a year, which means that the per capita consumption is a staggering 600 cups. The world's first commercial espresso machines were manufactured in Milan in the early years of the 20th century, but it was not until the 1930s that Francesco Illy developed an espresso machine that forced compressed air, rather than steam, through the grounds. In 1945 another Italian, Achille Gaggia, invented the spring-powered, piston-lever machine. The espresso brewing method allows the greatest amount of flavor and body to be extracted from the ground coffee, but this is done so quickly that the coffee has no time to become bitter or stale.

You can't go wrong if you use a Lavazza espresso blend.

Poster c. 1900, *Café Espresso by V. Ceccauti.*

Today's cafés offer an opportunity for a quick cup on the way to work. It is not unusual to see stylishly dressed office workers sipping their morning coffee from small china cups as they stand at the counters of the little espresso bars before they dash on to their work places.

The market leader is Lavazza, which has 45 percent of the market. In addition to its choice of ground coffees and beans, which are also available in Austria, France, Germany, the U.K., and the U.S., the company produces espresso machines. In the south of the country, the main seller is Kimbo, a Neapolitan company. The best-selling name in Rome is Classi Caffè Circi, followed by Peru, Illycaffè, and Iacocaffè. It seems that those living in the north prefer a lighter roast than the south.

Italian design has always been in the vanguard. One of the leading names in kitchen design is Alessi, which was founded in the 1920s in Crusinallo in northern Italy. It also has a "must-visit" factory store for anyone who is interested in the different ways of brewing and serving coffee.

Further south, in Rome, Nuova Point makes 15,000 espresso cups and saucers – nothing else – every day. If you have ever spent any time in an Italian espresso bar, this figure may not be altogether surprising. It has been estimated that in a busy inner-city espresso bar, a cup and saucer last, on average, for three months. The cups made by Nuova Point are just the right size, the inner section at the bottom collects the sugar and deposit, and the handles are easy to hold.

JAPAN

A cup of coffee in Tokyo can cost more than $50. It will usually be Jamaican Blue Mountain and will probably be served in the finest of bone-china cups.

Blue Mountain coffee is especially highly prized, and it is often given as a gift at New Year.

Japan may be the only country in the world to celebrate an official Coffee Day – it falls on October 1.

Espresso is not widely drunk, largely because the Japanese prefer light-roast beans. In addition, dairy products are not as popular among the Japanese as among Europeans, and there is little interest in cappuccino.

Canned coffee, both hot and cold, is, however, enormously popular. One of the best-selling brands is Kilimanjaro, which is made from Tanzanian beans (Tanzania is the sixth-largest coffee exporter to Japan). The canned market was worth $5.6 billion in 1992–3 – and this was at a time when the world green-bean trade, including Japanese imports, totaled $6 billion.

SWEDEN

The market share of Sweden's leading roasters is: Gevalia (General Foods AB) 30–35 percent; Cirkel AB (a cooperative) 20–25 percent; ICA Eosteri AB 15 percent; Anders Lofberg AB 15 percent; Zeogas Kaffe AB 10 percent; Arvid Norquist AB 5 percent.

UNITED KINGDOM

England is, above all, a tea-drinking nation, second only to Ireland in its per-capita consumption of tea, but when it comes to coffee, statistics show that 80 percent of consumption is of instant – which presents something of a challenge for the lovers of the real thing. General Foods recently found that retail sales of coffee in the U.K. stood at about £100 million more than tea, with the premium-market sector taking 11 percent by value.

One of the leading names in coffee in the U.K. is H. R. Higgins. Starting a business during World War II must have required something of an act of faith, but that is exactly what Harold Higgins did in 1942 when he opened a coffee store at 43 South Molton Street in London. The store had its own roaster and a supply of beans, closely regulated by the Ministry of Food. Although coffee was not rationed during the war, supplies were, necessarily, restricted and the selection was limited. Harold was later joined in the business by his son, Tony, and daughter, Audrey.

By the 1950s, trade and currency restrictions had eased, and more original coffees had become available. At this time,

David Higgins of H. R. Higgins Ltd,
specialist coffee merchants.

too, the popularity of coffee bars, which sprang up throughout Britain's major cities, did much to promote the image of coffee, especially among the young. Tea increasingly began to be associated with older people, while coffee was perceived to be a drink for the sophisticated young and associated with the European taste – the gleaming glass and brass espresso machines, introduced by Italians, heralded a sense of rebellion among the young.

As in other countries, small local roasters closed down as consumers increasingly bought branded coffees. Some of these roasters provided excellent coffee; many did not. However, there has always been a good supply of coffee available by mail order in the U.K., and Higgins now sells all his products this way. The original store has now become part of a designer-clothes pedestrian walkway, but Higgins now has a store in Duke Street, Mayfair. The firm is coffee supplier by Appointment to Her Majesty the Queen. Roasting is no longer carried on in the store, but in a specialist building outside London. The London store has a café in its basement, re-markable for serving only tea and coffee, no food, and for offering two cookies with each cup. The store on the ground floor retains the dark, traditional style of the early store, and, in a further link with the old traditions, the bags of coffee are tied with string.

Exterior of the shop in Duke Street, Mayfair, London.

The espresso market in the U.K. is the fastest-growing sector of the ground coffee market – it grew by 17 percent in 1993 – and Lavazza, which commands the largest share of the espresso market, is expanding aggressively in the U.K., including into the roast and ground market.

UNITED STATES

Most of the coffee drunk in the United States today comes from Brazil, Mexico, Colombia, and Guatemala. Although in general the U.S. is not a nation of quality coffee drinkers, there is a large and growing market that appreciates gourmet coffees. In the 1960s the situation was very different, for the market, concentrated in the hands of a few suppliers, was saturated with poor-quality coffee.

Typical mobile espresso/cappuccino cart, Seattle.

One of the problems facing the specialist coffee suppliers is the fact that espresso is not the ideal way of enjoying gourmet coffee. Although it is possible to drink highly roast or mid-roast coffee made on an espresso machine, it tastes better made by a longer infusion method. Espresso machines are ideal for high-mid to dark-dark roasts, and it is not necessary to use the very best coffees. When the coffee is high roast, its more subtle flavors are lost, as can be seen if an Ethiopian Harrar bean is used in an espresso machine.

Espresso coffee is, however, the most-often-offered cup, and there has been an enormous growth in the number of mobile espresso bars. An espresso service operation requires only low investment and often, sadly, not too much training. In California especially, perhaps because of the weather, there has been a huge increase in the number of espresso carts – mobile espresso-cappuccino bars, that offer quick service, often on a street corner, but also within shopping malls. Espresso and cappuccino are drunk on the move, from white paper cups with plastic lids.

The espresso beans consumed in the U.S. may require a higher roast because of the national taste for 100 percent arabica beans in espresso. In Italy and France, for example, the proportion of arabica to robusta is usually closer to 80:20. When arabica beans are low-dark roasted, they tend to release more acidity into the brew, so they usually have to be extra-high roasted to balance this acidity.

More strongly flavored beans are increasingly popular in the U.S., and this has manifested itself in a preference for darker-roasted beans. Some coffee connoisseurs regret this, because it becomes harder, rather than easier, to distinguish subtleties of flavor in dark-roast beans.

Consumer demand for gourmet coffees in the U.S. is expected to continue to grow, at least until the end of the decade, when the Specialty Coffee Association of America expects sales to achieve $3 billion. The main consumers of gourmet coffee have been identified as young, highly paid people who live in cities; 64 percent are likely to earn more than $50,000 a year. The Association believes that the estate origins of the coffees will become increasingly important and that flavored coffees will continue to increase their market share. Espresso bars and cafés are also expected to continue to grow, and it is thought that there may be as many as 1,400 mini-roasteries by the year 1999.

The Allegro Coffee Company, supplying good-quality coffee, is based in Boulder, Colorado, and was founded in 1977.

The founder's grandfather had, in fact, estab-

Allegro's products include carefully selected organic coffee.

──────── STARBUCKS ────────

THE COFFEE "REVOLUTION" began in the 1970s in Seattle, possibly because that city enjoys good, clean water, and Starbucks quickly became the city's second most famous export (Boeing being the first). The company was founded in 1970 by Gordon Bowker (whose idea it was), Jerry Baldwin, and Zev Siegl, and they took the name from Herman Melville's novel *Moby-Dick*, in which Starbuck is the first mate on the whaler *Pequod*. Zev Siegl went to Berkeley to train with Alfred Peet, who had coffee and tea experience from around the world and from whom, initially, Starbucks bought roasted coffees. In 1972 a second Starbucks store was opened and a secondhand roaster bought. At this time, too, a fourth partner joined the company, Jim Reynolds.

The company began to grow, and in 1990, Starbucks, which is nicknamed the Great Latte, moved outside Seattle and opened stores in Denver, Chicago, and Washington. The company went public in 1992, raising around $110 million, much of which will be invested in opening 225 new outlets. Sales for 1992 stood at $93 million and are

Starbucks CARE sampler; a portion of the price is passed on to CARE, the international aid and relief organisation.

Branch of Starbucks on Fillmore Street, San Francisco.

projected to rise to $240 million in 1994. In mid-1994, Starbucks was selling 800,000 cups of coffee a day.

Today Starbucks sells only coffees that it has roasted itself, and its coffeeshops serve coffee to drink on the spot, and sell both beans to take away and a wide selection of coffee making machines and accessories.

Starbucks seems less concerned with offering a quick "pick-me-up" for shoppers than with offering a better cup of coffee, a view that seems to be borne out by its comparatively small range of flavored coffees. Starbucks seems, in fact, to be more closely modeled on Italian coffee bars than on the traditional U.S. coffeeshop. Starbucks also has a reputation for roasting its coffee even darker than the darkest of the U.S. espresso roasters, thereby reducing the overall character of the coffee it sells. Consumer groups have commented on this, but the increasing numbers of customers passing through Starbucks' doors suggest that the consumers themselves like what they find there.

Lauren's Blend has a soft, smooth flavor and deep aftertaste.

Superior Coffee Company in Chicago in 1907, and Allegro continues to emphasize the importance of improvement and innovation while respecting the traditional roasting and blending techniques and recipes. Allegro imports only fine arabica beans and complements this side of the business with the provision of espresso and drip-coffee brewing technology. Another name synonymous with good coffee is Mountanos Brothers.

The largest U.S. coffee houses are Starbucks, Gloria Jean's Coffee Bean, Bernie's Coffee & Tea Co., and The Coffee Beanery Ltd.

KONA KAI FARMS COFFEE

Kona Kai Farms on the Kona Coast in Hawaii contains the only coffee grown in the United States, and it is coffee that is highly prized for its wonderful aroma and flavor. Coffee came to Kona in 1828 and did so well that it grew to be an economic mainstay of the Big Island. The 20-mile coffee belt is one of the world's finest areas for coffee – an ideal combination of temperature, soil, rain, and cloud cover exists to create greenhouse-like conditions. The flavor is unique – full bodied, slightly acid, mellow, and uncomplicated. Over the years, coffee has enjoyed periods of great popularity as well as having to endure sloughs. The emergence of Hawaii as the 50th state seemed to signal the end of a proud tradition, and by 1979 coffee production had slumped to 2,000 acres and 600 farms in Kona. The gourmet coffee industry has given Kona coffee a new lease of life, with the quest for exotic beans bringing a premium value to the beans that has justified the effort of farming the rugged, inhospitable land.

Global Coffee
Directory

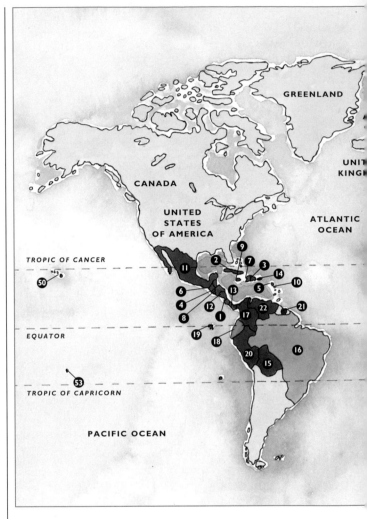

COFFEE PRODUCING
COUNTRIES OF THE WORLD

1 COSTA RICA	8 HONDURAS	16 BRAZIL
2 CUBA	9 JAMAICA	17 COLOMBIA
3 DOMINICAN	10 MARTINIQUE	18 ECUADOR
REPUBLIC	11 MEXICO	19 GALAPAGOS
4 EL SALVADOR	12 NICARAGUA	ISLANDS
5 GUADELOUPE	13 PANAMA	20 PERU
6 GUATEMALA	14 PUERTO RICO	21 SURINAM
7 HAITI	15 BOLIVIA	22 VENEZUELA

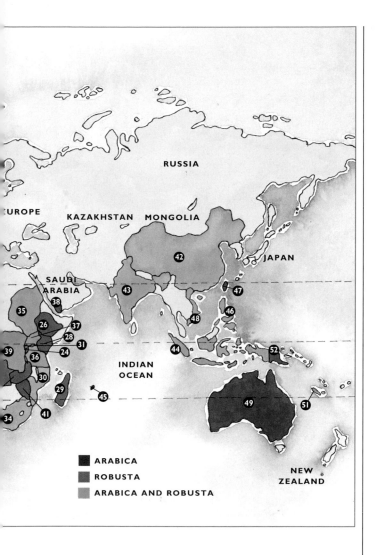

ARABICA

ROBUSTA

ARABICA AND ROBUSTA

23 ANGOLA	34 SOUTH AFRICA	45 LA REUNION
24 BURUNDI	35 SUDAN	46 PHILIPPINES
25 CAMEROON	36 TANZANIA	47 TAIWAN
26 ETHIOPIA	37 UGANDA	48 VIETNAM
27 IVORY COAST	38 YEMEN	49 AUSTRALIA
28 KENYA	39 ZAIRE	50 HAWAII
29 MADAGASCAR	40 ZAMBIA	51 NEW CALEDONIA
30 MOZAMBIQUE	41 ZIMBABWE	52 PAPUA NEW
31 RWANDA	42 CHINA	GUINEA
32 ST. HELENA	43 INDIA	53 TAHITI
33 SAO TOME AND PRINCIPE	44 INDONESIA	

This country-by-country guide covers the major coffee-producing countries in the world whose coffees are generally available to the general public, and also some minor countries who perhaps were once producing coffee and are no longer, or are still producing, but only on a very small scale. In these cases, it has been impossible to source any coffee to taste and so, unfortunately, there are no tasting notes.

INFORMATION BOXES

These boxes accompany each entry in the directory and give a brief description of the flavor of that particular coffee, a suggested roast (incorporating suggested uses where applicable) and finally, an overall star quality rating: fair, good, excellent. The star rating refers to the country as a whole and not to particular regions or estates.

FLAVOR	*full bodied with a lush, smoky flavor*
SUGGESTED ROAST	*medium to high; excellent for blending*
★ ★	*good*

FLAVOR PROFILE

This mini-table gives you at-a-glance information about the most important constituents that together make up the flavor. These are: body, acidity, and balance (see Tasting Coffee in the first part of the book for a full explanation of these terms).

FLAVOUR PROFILE

Body	🫘🫘🫘🫘🫘
Acidity	🫘🫘
Balance	🫘🫘🫘

CENTRAL AMERICA
AND THE
CARIBBEAN

COSTA RICA

Good acidity and a tangy aroma combined with full-bodied richness.

In many people's opinion, Costa Rican Tarrazu is one of the world's greatest coffees, with its light, clean flavor and wonderful fragrance.

Costa Rica, with its rich, well-drained, volcanic soil, was the first Central American country to grow coffee and bananas on a commercial basis, and both commodities are among its major exports. Coffee was introduced to Costa Rica, from Cuba, in 1729, and today the industry is one of the best organized in the world with a high yield of around 1,520 pounds per acre. The population of Costa Rica is 3.5 million, and there are 400 million coffee trees – not surprisingly, the good, highly consistent coffee represents about 25 percent of the country's export earnings. Costa Rica also benefits from the presence in Turrialba of the Central American Agricultural Research Institute (IAAC), which is an important international research center.

Unloading cherries from cart and oxen, Costa Rica

Only arabica beans are grown – growing robusta coffee is illegal. Good Costa Rican coffee is labeled "SHB" – strictly hard bean – which means that it been grown at an altitude above 5,000 feet. Altitude is often a problem for coffee growers. It is acknowledged that higher altitudes produce better beans, not only because they have the effect of increasing the acidity of the bean and thereby improving the flavor, but also because the cold nights that occur at the higher altitudes mean that the trees develop more slowly, which allows the beans to develop a fuller flavor. The regular rainfall that is caused by precipitation at the higher altitudes is also essential for the proper development of the trees. However, these advantages have to be offset against the additional transportation involved, which can increase costs to such an extent that the beans become uneconomical to produce. The Costa Rican industry has adopted new mechanical ways to improve efficiency, including the use of electric "eyes" to sort beans and identify irregularly sized beans.

Just south of the capital, San José, is the Tarrazu, one of the country's most highly regarded coffee-growing areas. Coffee labeled "La Minita Tarrazu" is produced in limited quantities – about 160,000 pounds each year – on an estate called La Minita and owned, for the last three generations, by Britain's McAlpine family. The estate, in fact, produces more than a million pounds of coffee a year, but the La Minita Tarrazu is grown without the use of artificial fertilizers or pesticides, and it is harvested and sorted separately and by hand, to obviate the criticism leveled at air-jet sorting, which is said to sometimes damage beans.

Other good names to look out for are Juan Vinas (PR), H. Tournon, Windmill (SHB), Montebellow, and Santa Rosa; and fine coffee is grown in Heredia and in the central valley. Another name to watch for is Sarchi, which is just one of five towns representing Costa Rica's "road of coffee." FJO Sarchi is grown on the slopes of the Poas volcano, which is about 33 miles from San José. The Sarchi company was founded in 1949, and now covers 76,000 acres. Sugarcane is grown there as well as coffee, and the region has become famous for its handicrafts, which attracts visitors from around the world.

The country's coffee industry was controlled by the Instituto del Cafe de Costa Rica (ICAFE), but this has been superceded by the Oficina del Cafe. All potential coffee exports that are not deemed to be of sufficiently high quality are dyed with blue vegetable dye and sold for domestic consumption, which, dyed blue or not, accounts for about 10 percent of total production and local consumption per capita is twice that of Italy or the U.S.

FLAVOR	excellent: silky with full acidity and accessible class; beguiling aroma
SUGGESTED ROAST	medium; can be high roasted
★ ★ ★	excellent

FLAVOR PROFILE

Body	🫘🫘🫘🫘
Acidity	🫘🫘🫘🫘🫘
Balance	🫘🫘🫘🫘

The FJO Sarchi estate produces one of Costa Rica's best coffees.

CUBA

It would be surprising if Cuba did not produce good coffee to accompany its fine cigars.

The best Cuban coffee is Turquino or Extra Turquino – Turquino is a grade rather than a district (such as Blue Mountain). The coffee is clean-tasting and medium-bodied, and it has a lower acidity than many of the coffees grown in Central America because it is grown at a lower altitude.

The future of Cuban coffee cannot be foretold. Certainty of supply and consistent quality cannot be assured in the present political climate. However, once these problems have been resolved, there is no doubt that Cuba could become an important source for both the U.S. and Japan.

FLAVOR	*full bodied with a lush, smoky flavor*
SUGGESTED ROAST	*medium to high; excellent for blending*
★ ★	*good*

FLAVOR PROFILE

Body	🫘🫘🫘
Acidity	🫘🫘
Balance	🫘🫘🫘

ATLANTIC OCEAN

Havana

Pinar Del Rio   Cien Fuegos

CUBA

Camaguey

Holguin

CARIBBEAN SEA

Santiago de Cuba

DOMINICAN REPUBLIC

*Coffee which is pleasantly sweet
and has good body.*

The Dominican Republic shares the island of Hispaniola with Haiti, and, like its neighbor, the country has had a history of revolution and poverty, although democratic elections have been held and some stability has been introduced.

Coffee was first grown in the Dominican Republic in the early 18th century. The best producing region is the southwest, in the region of Barahona, but fine coffee is also grown in Juncalito and Ocoa. The coffees, which are sometimes called Santo Domingo, provide good value for money, for they are mild and full-bodied, with good acidity and a pleasing aroma. Unlike the coffee produced in Haiti, most of the coffee produced in the Dominican Republic is washed, which is an indication of its high overall quality.

FLAVOR PROFILE

Body	● ●
Acidity	● ● ●
Balance	● ● ● ●

FLAVOR	*balanced with fair acidity*
SUGGESTED ROAST	*medium to high roast, good, all-round coffee with many uses*
★ ★	*good*

EL SALVADOR

*Exclusively arabica coffee which
is mild in flavor.*

Not only is El Salvador one of the smallest countries in the area, it is also one of the most densely populated. It produces balanced, if not distinctive coffee, which today accounts for about 40 percent of the country's exports. The best coffee is exported between January and March, with Germany taking 35 percent of the finest quality, the SHG.

Unfortunately, the recent guerilla war, as well as disrupting the nation's economy generally, did much, indirectly, to encourage the spread of coffee rust and coffee borer, and production fell from around 3½ million bags in the early 1970s to about 2½ million in 1990–1. The eastern parts of the country were affected the worst, causing many farmers and workers to flee from the plantations. Lack of investment has been reflected in a fall from the previously recorded very high yields of 1,080 pounds per acre to less than 800 pounds per acre today.

In addition to these problems, in 1986 the government imposed an additional 15 percent tax on exported coffee – this was in addition to an existing levy of 30 percent – and this, combined with the unfavorable exchange rate, led to a severe diminution in output and a sharp fall in quality.

However, in belated recognition of the fact that coffee is crucial to the national economy in terms of employment, foreign exchange earnings, and agricultural production, the recently elected government has taken steps to rectify the situation. In 1990 it partially privatized the coffee export industry in the hope that this will have the effect of increasing the availability of the coffee in export markets.

The coffee is typical of Central America – it is light-bodied, aromatic, clean, and has light acidity. As in Guatemala and Costa Rica, coffee is graded according to altitude – the higher the altitude, the better. The best-known brand name is Pipil, an Aztec-Mayan name for coffee, which is recognized by the Organic Certified Institute of America. An unusual bean is the Pacamara, a hybrid of the Pacas and *Maragogype*, and the best production is in the west of the country, around Santa Ana which is close to the border with Guatemala. Pacamara gives an exceptionally fine cup of coffee, which is full-bodied, but not too heavy and fragrant.

Packing coffee beans for export, Cuscachapa, El Salvador.

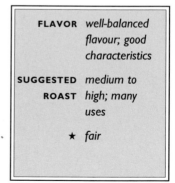

FLAVOR	well-balanced flavour; good characteristics
SUGGESTED ROAST	medium to high; many uses
★	fair

FLAVOR PROFILE

Body	🟤🟤
Acidity	🟤🟤
Balance	🟤🟤🟤

GUADELOUPE

*Good coffee production succumbs
to natural disasters.*

This group of islands in the Caribbean used to be a significant producer. In 1789, 4,000 tons were produced from over a million trees planted on about 200 acres of land. Today, only about 60 acres are devoted to producing coffee.

The reasons for this decline may be traced to the increased production of sugarcane and bananas and the damage done to the coffee trees in 1966 by Hurricane Ines. Political reasons include a reallocation of land that was carried out in 1962–5, which did great damage to the coffee production, which is both more labor-intensive and capital-hungry than both banana and sugarcane cultivation.

Almost no coffee is exported from Guadeloupe now, although it used to be among the best grown in the area. The finest quality is classified as Bonifieur, a name that is honored in the history of coffee.

GUATEMALA

The strictly high bean is full-bodied and deliciously balanced – a spicy, complex cup.

Guatemalan coffee once enjoyed a reputation for being one of the very best available. For a while, however, quality slipped; happily it is now regaining its former glory.

Coffee trees were introduced to the country in 1750 by Jesuit priests, and the industry was developed by German settlers in the late 19th century. Today, most production is carried out in the south of the country, where the slopes of the volcanic mountains in the Sierra Madre provide ideal conditions for fine-quality arabica beans. The high altitude produces wonderfully lively coffee, and connoisseurs often prefer the spicy, complex flavor to other kinds of bean. The SHB coffee is among the best you can find – full-bodied with deliciously balanced acidity. Elephant beans have earned Guatemala a lot of attention, although many people believe that the quality is not what it used to be.

Coffee initially made the country prosperous, and still dominates the economy. Unfortunately, however, the political situation within the country has not benefitted the coffee growers. Yields, which are often a good indication of a country's overall economy, are comparatively low at 625 pounds per acre. In El Salvador, on the other hand, the yield is 800 pounds per acre, and in Costa Rica it is an astonishing 1,520 pounds per acre. The export trade is in the hands of private companies, but the Asociacion Nacional de Cafe (Anacafe) controls all other aspects of the industry. Minimum daily wages throughout the country have recently been increased from $1.74 to $2.51 – and this is at a time when some of the best Guatemalan coffees are exported to Japan, where they sell for the equivalent of $3–4.00 per cup.

Most of the smaller producers are of Mayan descent – they prefer to be called *naturales* – and they are at present benefiting from a U.S.-funded program, known locally as "The Project," which is investing $25 million to encourage small, gourmet production. The main areas of excellence are at Lake Atitlan and Huehuentenango. The Project aims to help overcome the cycle of high-yield, low-quality plants which besets coffee production throughout the world. Bourbon trees, for example, are taller growing and produce fewer beans than new varieties of dwarf trees, but, even though both are arabica, the bourbon trees produce finer beans and are, from the point of view of gourmet customers, preferable. The Project is also hoping to be able to encourage local producers to process their own beans. At present, most of the red cherries are sold to middlemen, but more added value and perhaps quality will result if processing is carried out in local mills.

FLAVOR	*full, attractive, spicy, and complete*
SUGGESTED ROAST	*medium; can be high roasted*
★ ★ ★	*excellent*

Coffee tree on the Guatemalan coast.

Names to look out for are Antigua, which is the best-known region. Among the coffees from Antigua is that produced on the Hacienda Carmona, whose best coffee is called El Pulcal, which is not only of excellent quality but has a fuller, smokier more complex flavor than other Guatemalan coffees. About every 30 years, the area around Antigua is subject to volcanic eruptions, which provide additional nitrogen to the already rich soil. The area is further blessed by light, frequent rainfall, and sun.

Other names worth looking out for are, as we have already noted, the coffees produced at Huehuentenango and around Lake Atitlan, as well as San Marco, Oriente and Coban, Palcya, Mataquescuintia, and La Uman in Zacapa. The authentication of gourmet coffee has only just begun, but the establishment of the Speciality Coffee Association of Guatemala should mean that progress in this area will soon be evident.

FLAVOR PROFILE

Body	🟤🟤🟤🟤
Acidity	🟤🟤🟤🟤
Balance	🟤🟤🟤🟤

HAITI

Good coffee from a politically troubled country.

Despite its well-publicized problems, Haiti manages to produce some good coffee, although the quality is variable.

Much of the coffee produced in Haiti is organic. This is less by design than by default, for the farmers are too poor to buy fungicides, pesticides, and fertilizers. The main growing area is in the north of the country, but, more than almost any other producer, Haiti has developed a multiplicity of names, classifications, and types.

Haitian coffee has the distinction of being used in Japan to add to Jamaica Blue Mountain to make it go further.

The coffee itself is heavy-bodied and quite full-flavored with mid to low acidity with a somewhat soft flavor.

FLAVOR	balanced and dense
SUGGESTED ROAST	medium; good high roast, especially for espresso
★	fair

FLAVOR PROFILE

Body	🫘🫘🫘🫘
Acidity	🫘🫘
Balance	🫘🫘🫘

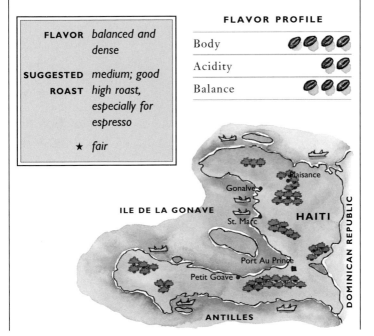

HONDURAS

Honduran coffee is generally a well-regarded, blending coffee.

Coffee was brought to Honduras from El Salvador, and the country now produces good-quality coffee, often with good acidity.

As elsewhere, classification depends on altitude. In Honduras coffee grown at 2,300–3,280 feet is known as Central Standard, that grown at 3,280–4,900 feet is known as High Grown, and that grown at 4,900–6,560 feet is Strictly High Grown. After the Brazilian frost of 1975, production increased significantly – from 500,000 bags to 1.8 million bags in 20 years.

Coffee rust has proved to be a hazard, especially in the east of the country. The copper sprays used to treat this disease have had the unexpected benefit of increasing yields. All the coffee is exported by private shippers, and most of it to the U.S. and Germany.

FLAVOR	good, soft; useful for blending and as a single
SUGGESTED ROAST	medium to high; many uses
★ ★	good

FLAVOR PROFILE

Body	🫘🫘🫘
Acidity	🫘🫘🫘🫘
Balance	🫘🫘🫘🫘

JAMAICA

Is Jamaica Blue Mountain the best coffee in the world?

Almost everyone who has heard of Jamaica Blue Mountain knows that it is the most expensive coffee in the world, but not everyone knows why. When an article – whether it is a Rolls-Royce or a Stradivarius violin – acquires a reputation as being "the best in the world," the reputation tends to develop a life of its own, and it becomes something of a self-perpetuating myth. In a complicated world, a simplification is often welcome.

At its best, there can be no doubt that Blue Mountain is one of the very best coffees available. The price, however, does not reflect the "better" flavor as much as the premium that some people are prepared to pay to secure supplies of it. It is also worth remembering that this coffee is even more expensive to drink than it seems – to enjoy the flavor at its best, you have to use more beans per cup than for other coffees. If you do not, the flavor can seem a little hollow. So the real cost of the flavor is the difference between it and the next most expensive coffee, plus 10 or 15 percent for the extra beans needed.

That said, however, real Blue Mountain coffee, which comes from the appropriately best local blue-green beans, is a connoisseur's delight. The flavor is full: it has balance, fruit, and acidity and provides all the satisfaction one could want. The aroma is intense and strong, but above all the flavor of good, fresh Blue Mountain is unusually persistent and, as wine drinkers might say, develops on the palate.

It is worth looking closely at the myth of Blue Mountain, for past image and present reality are not always the same. The first trees were brought to Jamaica from Martinique in 1725. They were imported by Sir Nicholas Lawes and planted in St. Andrew parish, which is still one of the three Blue Mountain parishes, the other two being Portland and St. Thomas. Within eight years, more than 83,000 pounds of clean beans were being exported. Production peaked in 1932 when more than 33 million pounds were grown.

By 1948, however, the quality of the coffee had deteriorated to such an extent that Canadian buyers refused to renew their contracts, and the Jamaican government established the Coffee Industry Board to revive the industry's fortunes. By 1969 matters had improved sufficiently for Japanese loans to be offered to improve production quality and to guarantee a market. Even in 1969, Japanese coffee drinkers were willing to pay a premium price for this coffee – and today it enjoys something approaching cult status.

Jamaica Blue Mountain green beans.

By 1981 a further 3,500 acres or so had been brought into cultivation, and this was followed by the financing of an additional 15,000 acres. Today the Blue Mountain region is, in fact, only a tiny growing area of around 15,000 acres, and it is impossible for all the coffee labeled "Blue Mountain" to have originated there. A further 30,000 acres produces two main classifications of non-Blue Mountain coffee – High Mountain Supreme and Prime Washed Jamaican.

True Blue Mountain coffee is one of the highest grown coffees in the world, and the climate, geology, and topology of Jamaica combine to provide the ideal location. The spine of mountains that runs across Jamaica ends in the east of the island in the Blue Mountains, which reach to over 7,000 feet. The climate is cool and misty, with frequent rainfall, and the rich soil is well drained. Terracing and mixed cropping are used, with coffee growing alongside bananas and avocados.

It is available from small estates such as the Wallenford Estate, the Silver Hill Estate, or from the Atlanta estate of J. Martinez. Even the largest growers in the area are small by international standards, and many are small plot-holders, whose families have worked the land for two centuries. The industry faces problems from increasing labor costs and from the fact that the nature of the terrain makes mechanization difficult. The numerous small estates and farms also makes rationalization of production difficult. Jamaica is also prone to hurricanes.

Blue Mountain is, nevertheless, the one coffee that all self-respecting coffee retailers stock. One leading retailer in Britain reports selling it consistently throughout the year, despite the price: "We have customers who will buy nothing less."

The Japanese now buy up to 90 percent of the crop. In 1992 that meant 688 tons, compared with 75 tons sold to the U.S. and 59 tons to the U.K. With only 10 percent available for the rest of the world there is always going to be a shortfall, whatever the price. In the U.K., Langford Brothers was, for many years, the only supplier. Recently, the Edmonds Group has begun to obtain supplies of Blue Mountain from a Jamaican company, Salda Foods.

Blue Mountain is distinguished from other coffees by being transported in wooden barrels that contain 154 pounds. The barrels – which were copied from the *Bonifieur* produced on Guadeloupe in the the last century and were originally the barrels in which flour had been sent to Jamaica from Britain – always bear the brand names or appellations of the processing factory. The Coffee Industry Board certifies all pure Jamaican coffee and issues a seal of authenticity before it is exported.

The Jamaican government used to insist that all Blue Mountain coffee was roasted in Jamaica ostensibly so that it could guarantee that quality was maintained. In fact, roasting is a fine art, and doing it well requires experience, training, and expensive equipment. From a consumer's point of view, coffee beans should be acquired and used as soon after roasting as possible, conditions that are unlikely to be met by the coffee having been roasted in Jamaica. Fortunately, green beans can now be exported.

FLAVOR	very full, with prominent fruit flavors
SUGGESTED ROAST	medium
★ ★ ★	excellent

FLAVOR PROFILE

Body	🫘🫘🫘🫘
Acidity	🫘🫘🫘
Balance	🫘🫘🫘🫘

Langford Brothers is an approved brand of Jamaica Blue Mountain coffee.

Langford Brothers Original 100% Pure
JAMAICA
BLUE MOUNTAIN

FILTER FINE GROUND
VACUUM PACKED
COFFEE

NET WEIGHT
℮ 8oz *226g*

Martinique

The cradle of American coffee.

The little island of Martinique was the original source of all the coffee in Central America, but today very little is produced there. The first coffee tree in the Western hemisphere was brought from France by Captain Gabriel Mathieu de Clieu in the early 1720s. De Clieu, a naval officer serving in Martinique, brought a tree and planted it in Prechear, where the first harvest was gathered in 1726. From Martinique, plants were sent to Haiti, the Dominican Republic, and Guadeloupe, and by 1777 it is recorded that there were 18,791,680 coffee plants in Martinique.

The story is a testimony to the growth of an industry and its destruction at the hands of national calamities and political incompetence, for today Martinique's exports are bananas, sugarcane, and pineapples.

MEXICO

Smooth, fragrant coffee from the fourth largest producer in the world.

The fourth largest coffee producer in the world, Mexico has an annual production of about 5 million bags. Most of the coffee is produced by around 100,000 smallholders, and the great estates that once dominated the industry are rare today. The average yield is about 560 pounds per acre, and until recently the industry was dominated by the Instituto Mexicano del Cafe (Inmecafe), which both controlled the areas planted with coffee and marketed the beans, which are available for export from November. Inmecafe offered a minimum price and supplied technical advice and other assistance to the farmers. Since 1991 the activities of Inmecafe have been somewhat curtailed, and its role may be still further reduced.

The collapse of the Coffee Agreement and the disappearance of price support has, actually, been of help to some producers because it has forced them to develop individual brands and to acquire closer relationships with their markets, both domestically and within the U.S. The NAFTA agreement between Canada, the U.S., and Mexico will further assist Mexican exports to North America.

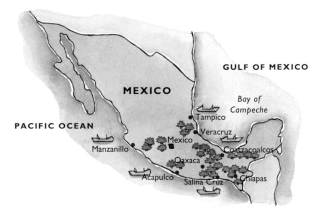

Farmer on a coffee plantation, Roma, Mexico.

Some people believe that the best of the elephant beans are produced in Mexico, not Guatemala, but both supply and quality are variable. The beans – known as *maragogype* – are large and give a smoothly mellow, fragrant coffee. Poverty among the farmers, rather than principle, means that much of the coffee is organically grown, but this is unregulated and largely unauthenticated.

The best region is Chiapas in the south of the country, where the brand names include Tapanchula and Huixtla. Oaxaca also produces fine beans, and the top name to look out for there is an organically grown bean, Pluma Coixtepec. Also from Oaxaca are Altura Orizaba and Altura Huatusco, while from Veracruz comes the Altura Coatapec. The best elephant bean to come from Mexico is known as Liquidambar MS.

FLAVOR PROFILE

Body	🫘🫘🫘🫘
Acidity	🫘🫘🫘🫘
Balance	🫘🫘🫘🫘

FLAVOR	smooth and fragrant with good, mellow depth of flavor
SUGGESTED ROAST	excellent as high roast
★ ★	very good

119

NICARAGUA

The very best Nicaraguan coffees are among the finest in the world – mild, mid-bodied, and very fragrant.

Political problems have, in so many countries, badly affected coffee production, and the Nicaraguan coffee industry has been no exception. The 1979 revolution caused the coffee plantation owners to flee to Miami, and there then followed a period of indecision while the government considered whether the land, including the coffee plantations, should be redistributed. This led to a disruption in supply, with production falling from over 1 million bags in the early 1970s to fewer than 600,000 in 1990.

The industry has now been freed from government restraint, and marketing is in the hands of private companies. The best Nicaraguan coffees are grown in the north and center of the country, and the best of all come from Matagalpa, Jinotega, and Nuevo Segovia.

The best Nicaraguan coffees, which are classified as Central Estrictamente Altura, are very satisfying, with good acidity and fine fragrance. The poorer-quality beans are widely used in blends.

FLAVOR	good blending beans; top-quality beans very fragrant
SUGGESTED ROAST	excellent high-roast beans; good for espresso
★	fair

FLAVOR PROFILE

Body	▨▨
Acidity	▨▨▨
Balance	▨▨▨

PANAMA

No estate-grown coffee is available yet, although the high-grown coffee is uniformly fine.

Coffee from Panama is famously smooth, light-bodied, and very balanced, and the top-quality beans offer real character and good flavor. Almost all of the best beans go to France and Finland, with the first shipments being made in November.

The finest beans are grown in the north of the country, near to the border with Costa Rica and on the Pacific side. The Boquet district in Chiriqui province produces notable coffee, and the other districts to look out for are David, Remacimeinto, Bugaba, and Tole.

A name for the future is Café Volcan Baru, which is a premium specialty coffee. 1994 production amounted to 2,000 bags, or 1 percent of Panama's total.

FLAVOR PROFILE

Body	🫘🫘🫘🫘
Acidity	🫘🫘🫘
Balance	🫘🫘🫘🫘

FLAVOR	good quality with full body
SUGGESTED ROAST	medium roast
★ ★	good

CARIBBEAN SEA

COSTA RICA

BOCAS DEL TORO

Cristobal

Panama City

Boquete

CHIRIQUI

PANAMA

Balboa

David

Tole

VERAGUAS

Santiago

HERRERA

PUERTO RICO

Yauco Selecto is one of the best coffees in the world.

Coffee trees were brought to Puerto Rico from Martinique in 1736, and their early cultivation was mostly carried out by Corsican immigrants. By 1896 Puerto Rico was the sixth leading exporter of coffee in the world, with most of the coffee going to France, Italy, Spain, and interestingly, Cuba. Although coffee plantations thrived in the 19th century, sugar and pharmaceutical products combined with hurricanes and war to push coffee into the background, but the industry is now being revived.

Puerto Rico is a commonwealth and an associated state of the U.S. As such, it has a policy of paying a minimum wage, which in 1991 was $4.20 an hour. Labor costs are, therefore, high compared with many other coffee-producing countries – only Hawaii and Jamaica face comparable labor costs. Another problem facing the coffee industry is that Puerto Ricans are among the best-educated people in the Caribbean and have appropriately high career expectations.

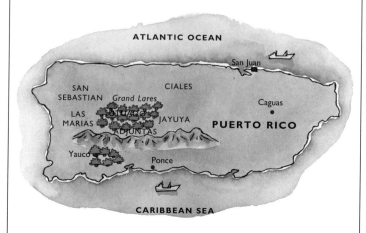

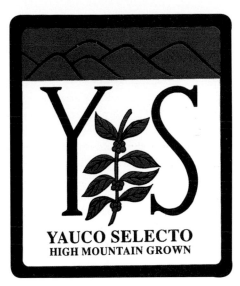

YAUCO SELECTO
HIGH MOUNTAIN GROWN

Gourmet estate coffee from Puerto Rico.

Today, gourmet coffees are exported to the U.S., France, and Japan. The country's coffee is generally carefully cultivated and has a mild flavor, heavy body and good aroma. The top-of-the-line coffees are among the best in the world, and the very best are Yauco Selecto (*selecto* means "chosen") and Grand Lares – Yauco is in the southwest of the island and Lares in the south-central area.

Yauco Selecto, which is grown on only three farms in the southwest of the island, is very full flavored, with an intense aroma and a unique after-taste. It is high in price, but the flavor is the equal of any in the world. The coffee is owned and managed by all the participating farmers in the Yauco region, whose mountain location offers a temperate climate and a longer maturation period, from October to February, together with a good, clay-based soil. Old styles of arabica beans are grown, and although the bourbon and Puerto Rican varieties give a lower yield than some other kinds, they give uniformly high quality. An ecological, worker-friendly approach to cultivation has been adopted, with low-toxicity chemicals and herbicides used. Employing mixed-use agriculture helps to enrich the soil. Only ripe beans are picked, which requires multiple passes through the coffee trees. The beans are then drum-washed for 48 hours.

Yauco Selecto is run on a "husk until shipment" basis, by which beans are dehusked only after an order has been placed, to guarantee maximum freshness. Alongside the commitment of the growers stand the various U.S. government agencies – the FDA and the USDA, for example – which monitor compliance with Federal rules. There are local tasting committees, and 1 bag out of every 50 is sampled by international cuppers.

The man behind all this attention to detail is Jaime Fortuño, the president of Escogido Yauco agents. An ex-investment banker and graduate of Harvard Business School, Señor Fortuño is determined that nothing will be left to chance in recreating a market for top-quality Puerto Rican coffee. Maximum production will be three thousand 100-pound bags each year, which is less than 1 percent of the island's total coffee production.

Yauco Selecto is a lovely coffee, with a full flavor and no bitterness. It is rich and fruity and well worth trying to find. In the U.K. Taylors of Harrogate is importing 50 bags of Peaberry Yauco Selecto.

YAUCO SELECTO
Café Gourmet de Puerto Rico

DELEITESE CON UNA LEYENDA PRECIADA, OTRA VEZ.

INDULGE IN A CHERISHED LEGEND AGAIN.

RENOUEZ AVEC DES DÉLICES LÉGENDAIRES.

GÖNNEN SIE SICH WIEDER EINE LEGENDÄRE DELIKATESSE.

FLAVOR	full bodied, sophisticated flavor; very aromatic
SUGGESTED ROAST	medium
★ ★ ★	excellent

FLAVOR PROFILE

Body	
Acidity	
Balance	

Promoting Puerto Rico's best coffee.

SOUTH AMERICA

BOLIVIA

*Coffee from the hedges in the garden
to the plantation.*

Coffee trees used to be planted in hedges on rural estates to provide floral decoration. Commercial production began in earnest only in the 1950s, and it received a boost from the frost that did so much damage to Brazil's coffee industry in 1975.

The coffee is high grown, at an altitude of between 600 and 2,200 feet above sea level, and the washed arabica beans are imported by Germany and Switzerland. The flavor is not of the very finest quality found nowadays and has a tendency toward bitterness.

FLAVOR PROFILE

Body	🫘🫘🫘
Acidity	🫘🫘
Balance	🫘🫘

FLAVOR	*good blending coffee*
SUGGESTED ROAST	*medium to high*
★	*fair*

BRAZIL

*Medium-roast beans with low acidity from the center
of the coffee world.*

As the song says, they do have a lot of coffee in Brazil, and the country has been accurately described as the "giant, the monarch" of the coffee world. There are, for example, some 3,970 million coffee trees in Brazil, with small farmers now accounting for about 75 percent of the country's production. It is perhaps worth noting that there are two or three times as many coffee producers in Brazil as there are in the world's second largest producer, Colombia.

Today, Brazil's economy is less dependent on coffee than at one time, and it now represents only 8–10 percent of the country's gross domestic product. Before World War II, Brazil's share of world production was over 50 percent; it is

now nearer to 30 percent. The country's effect on the world of coffee, especially on the price of coffee, is however second to none, with two frosts in 1994 precipitating steep rises in world coffee prices.

Coffee production has become something of a science since coffee trees were introduced to Brazil from French Guyana in 1720. Until 1990 the industry was very tightly regulated and controlled, with stringent interventionist and price-protection measures. Minimum prices to farmers were maintained by the state, which bought up surpluses. At one stage before World War II, surplus stocks amounted to 78 million bags, which were destroyed by fire or by immersion.

Since 1990 a free market has operated. The old Instituto Brasileiro do Cafe (IBL) has been replaced by the non-interventionist Secreteria Nacional de Economia, and producers are allowed to negotiate prices directly with exporters. The exporters' activities are, however, regulated by the government, which maintains a register of approved exporters.

Nursery stock in Brazil.

FLAVOR	*many variations available, but generally soft and mild with low acidity*
SUGGESTED ROAST	*light to high; many styles and qualities for all uses*
★ ★	*good*

FLAVOR PROFILE

Body	🫘🫘🫘
Acidity	🫘🫘
Balance	🫘🫘🫘

Coffee warehouse in Brazil.

To call a coffee "Brazilian" is meaningless, given the huge number of different kinds available. In the coffee market, Brazilian coffee, which is mostly unwashed and sun dried, is called "Brazils" to distinguish it from "Milds," as are other arabicas. The beans are further classified by the name of the state in which they were produced and by the port through which they were shipped. Although coffee is grown in 17 of Brazil's 21 states, four of those states – Parana, Sao Paulo, Minas Gerais, and Espirito Santo – produce 98 percent of the total production, with Parana state in the south alone being responsible for an astonishing 50 percent of the overall production.

Given the diversity of the industry, there is a Brazilian coffee to suit all tastes. The northern seaboard area, for example, produces coffee that has the typical iodized flavor reminiscent of the sea, and this kind of coffee is sold to North Africa, the Middle East, and Eastern Europe.

One of the most interesting coffees, and one that is worth tracking down, is washed Bahia. This is not easy to find because, after the United States, Brazil is the largest coffee con-

sumer in the world, and many fine coffees find their way into the home market.

The country produces the largest volume of the ordinary robusta that is used in supermarket coffee. Brazilian robusta is marketed under the name Conillon, and it represents 15 percent of total production.

However, in the southeast, in the state of Minas Gerais, some estates in the Cerrado region have found old bourbon plants, and coffee from these estates – Capin Branco and Vista Allegre, for example – is now being offered. Although from the same area, these coffees are very different in character – Capin Branco is smoother than Vista Allegre, which is spicy and brambly. Both have relatively low acidity, but, like all Brazilian coffees, they are best drunk young, because they tend to develop excessive acidity with age. Growers have organized themselves into the Speciality Coffee Association of Brazil.

Poster by Lois Gaigg, 1987.

COLOMBIA

*The largest producer of quality coffee in the world –
traditional dark-roast coffee with a strong,
memorable flavor.*

Coffee was first introduced to Colombia in 1808, when
trees were brought by a clergyman from the French Antilles
via Venezuela. Today the country is the second largest producing country in the world after Brazil, with an annual production of 13 million 130-pound bags compared with Brazil's
22 million bags. The importance of coffee to the national
economy may be gauged from the fact that all cars entering
the country are sprayed so that they do not inadvertently
introduce diseases that might damage the coffee plants.

Picking coffee cherries in Colombia during harvesting season.

Colombian coffee is one of the few original coffees sold all over the world under its own name. No other coffee has achieved that degree of consumer regard for its quality. It is the world's largest exporter of arabica beans – very little robusta is grown – and the world's largest exporter of washed beans. More than any other producer, the country has been concerned to develop and promote its product and industry, and it is this, together with favorable geographical and climatic factors, that has given Colombian its reputation for quality and flavor.

The coffee-producing areas lie among the foothills of the Andes, where the climate is temperate and moist. Colombia has three *cordilleras* – secondary mountain ranges – running through it, north to south, toward the Andes proper, and it is along the heights of the *cordilleras* that the coffee is grown. The hilly terrain provides a wide variety of microclimates, which mean that the harvesting season can last for almost the whole year, as different plantings ripen at different times. Colombia is also fortunate in that, unlike Brazil, it does not have to worry about the possibility of frost destroying a crop. There are around 2,700 million coffee trees, about 66 percent being grown on plantations organized on modern lines, with the remainder being grown on small, traditionally run farms.

FLAVOR PROFILE

Body	🫘🫘🫘
Acidity	🫘🫘🫘
Balance	🫘🫘🫘🫘🫘

FLAVOR	*rich; superbly balanced; sometimes nutty*
SUGGESTED ROAST	*medium to high; all uses*
★ ★ ★	*excellent*

Yields have risen from around 1,500 pounds per acre in the early 1960s to around 2,000 pounds per acre today, and some exceptional farms can achieve yields of 4,000 pounds per acre. However, maintaining quality is a priority for the industry, which is managed by the Federacion Nacional de Cafeteros (FNC), which was founded in 1927. Although it is a private company, the FNC acts with the government. In addition to organizing the industry, it builds up reserves of money in the good years, although in the last few years, when coffee prices have tended to fall, even the FNC ran out of cash. In general, however, the FNC offers health care and education, builds roads, employs agronomists, carries out research, regulates quality, directly exports half of the total export volume, and employs marketing agents. Like Kenya, it is a model for how the industry can be organized.

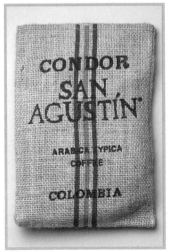

Quality and flavorsome coffee from Colombia.

Coffee seed bed in Colombia.

The coffee farmers can either sell the entire crop to the FNC at the official minimum price or sell to exporters, who may offer a higher price – or no price at all. In practice, the FNC dominates exports to Europe, while supplies to the U.S. are handled through the private exporters. All exports, however, are subject to a minimum export price, the *reintegro cafetero*.

Colombia is fortunate in having both Atlantic and Pacific ports – the only South American country to do so – and this helps to keep down transportation and shipping costs. The main production areas are along the central and eastern *cordilleras*, and along the central range the most important plantations are at Medellin, Armenia, and Manizales. Of the three, the coffee from Medellin is the finest – it has a heavy body, a rich, full flavor, and medium acidity. The three areas are known collectively as MAM from the names of the main towns, and most of the top quality Colombian coffee available for export is probably MAM. Coffee from Medellin alone would be so identified, and premium prices would be charged. Along the eastern *cordillera*, the two best areas are those around Bogotá and, further north, around Bucaramanga. Coffee from Bogotá is less acidic than that from Medellin, but is equally fine.

Germany imports 25 percent of all Colombian coffee exports, which is an indication of its consistent quality. The coffee is graded as Supremo; Excelso (of which Klauss is exported to Germany; Europa to France, Spain, and Italy; and Scandinavian to the north European countries); and UGQ, which stands for "Unusual Good Quality." It is possible to buy both Excelso and Supremo in many coffee shops. The "official" difference between the two is that Supremo tends to have the larger beans. In fact, Supremo tends to come from the more up-to-date producers, where consistent quality is easier to maintain. Excelso is often softer and more acidic than Supremo, but both are aromatic coffees, with medium body and good fruit. Colombian coffee is often described as silky, and it is one of the best balanced of all coffees and one that can be drunk at any time of the day.

The great dilemma facing Colombian coffee producers is whether to replace the bourbon trees with faster-growing, high-yielding species of arabica trees. Some say that the quality will not be so good; others say that in the best coffee-growing areas, the difference will be slight.

ECUADOR

*Perhaps the highest arabica plantations
in the world.*

Arabica trees were first planted in Ecuador as recently as 1952. The coffee is of good quality, especially if it comes from the early June crop and not from a later harvest.

The beans are classified as Galapagos and Gigante, both of which are heavy and large, and as No. 1 and Extra Superior, which are of Scandinavian consumer quality.

The main problems confronting producers is maintaining a consistent quality. Nevertheless, the coffee is generally well balanced and clean, and has an excellent, somewhat individual, aroma.

Ecuador is one of the few countries in South America to produce robusta as well as arabica, although the production of robusta is increasing because of the lack of suitable land for the arabica trees. The best of the arabica coffee comes from the high lands of the Andes, which run in two ranges from north to south down the center of the country, especially from the Chanchamgo Valley.

FLAVOR	balanced with vibrant flavors
SUGGESTED ROAST	medium to high; good blending coffee; versatile
★	fair

FLAVOR PROFILE

Body	🫘🫘
Acidity	🫘🫘🫘
Balance	🫘🫘🫘🫘

GALAPAGOS ISLANDS

A coffee rarity from the home of the giant tortoise.

This rare and unusual coffee is of very high quality and is grown without the use of chemicals of any kind.

The coffee is grown on San Cristóbal, one of the larger islands in the archipelago and the only island in the group with an abundance of fresh water. Streams, fed by a lagoon known as El Junco, which lies 1,350 feet above sea level, flow down the rocky, volcanic slopes of the island's southerly side. This mineral-rich fresh water keeps the soil moist and fertile.

In 1875 Mañuel J. Cobos, a native of Ecuador, planted about 250 acres of arabica bourbon coffee on the Hacienda El Cafetal on San Cristóbal. The plantation is located at between 450 and 900 feet above sea level, which is the atmospheric equivalent of 3,000 to 6,000 feet above sea level on the mainland. These elevations are ideally suited to the growth of

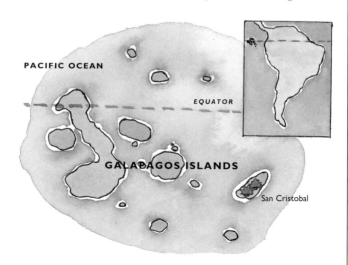

strictly hard bean – SHB – with its high acidity, and they are the key to the high quality of the coffee produced there.

As the world's coffee industry evolved to a more volume-oriented business, the small, quality-conscious industry on San Cristóbal fell on hard times, and was eventually abandoned as unprofitable. In the early 1990s, however, the Gonzalez family purchased the Hacienda El Cafetal. The unique opportunity offered by the microclimate created by the Humboldt Current, the intense equatorial sun, and the dramatic climate change that occurs as the climate increases – 110°F at sea level; 50–60°F at 900 feet – encouraged the Gonzalez family to expand the plantation.

Since then, the plantation has doubled in size, through the recultivation of earlier cultivated ground. Because of their unique role in the history of evolution, the government of Ecuador has made the Galapagos Islands a national park, and no new land may be taken into agricultural use. In addition, the importation and use of fertilizers, pesticides, herbicides, and any other chemicals is strictly prohibited, so Galapagos Island coffee is unofficially, if not officially, categorized as organic.

Annual production of this rarity currently amounts to 500 bags of grade II coffee. The Gonzalez family hopes to be able to increase production in the years ahead to as much as 5,000 bags, of which 50 percent will be grade I quality.

FLAVOR	*rich with a sweet acidity*
SUGGESTED ROAST	*full to medium*
★ ★ ★	*excellent*

FLAVOR PROFILE

Body	🫘🫘🫘🫘
Acidity	🫘🫘🫘
Balance	🫘🫘🫘

PERU

Good, balanced coffee that can be used in blends.

Peru is one of the great "could-be" coffee stories, for given the right economic conditions and political stability it could grow excellent coffee.

As much as 98 percent of all Peruvian coffee is grown in the forested areas, and most of the growers are small peasant farmers. The local problems are, however, extensive. Apart from the guerilla war and the activities of the Sondero Luminosa ("Shining Path") and drug traffickers, the recent appearance of cholera in the coastal zone has caused still further disruption. On top of this is the fact that inflation has reached an annual rate of 7,000 percent.

In the mid-1970s, production was around 900,000 bags per year, and this has been steadily increased to an annual output of about 1.3 million bags. The marketing is a government

monopoly, although private exporters operate through inter-mediaries to collect coffee grown in the most far-flung areas. Recently the Comera de Exportadores de Cafe del Peru was founded, and this private company has been working hard to improve quality. Its first task has been to attempt to regulate standards by identifying defects and striving to instill a "culture" of quality. This positive move bodes well for the future, as does the recent rise in prices, which should encourage farmers to plant coffee trees rather than the other traditional cash crop of the area, cocoa.

The best coffee comes from Chancimayo, Cuzco, Norte, and Puno. A large proportion of Peruvian coffee is sold as "organic," and this itself is problematical, for it is difficult, if not impossible, to authenticate the growing conditions of all coffee trees. Organically grown beans can command a 10–20 percent premium in terms of price, and, given the widespread poverty, it would seem entirely likely that farmers would not be able to buy fertilizers and pesticides. Nevertheless, there is still the problem of verifying the status of the whole crop.

Peruvian coffee can be as good as any other Central or South American coffee. Indeed, the best of the coffee that is produced is sent to Germany for blending and to Japan and the U.S., which indicates its high standard.

FLAVOR	*balanced with valued acidity*
SUGGESTED ROAST	*medium to high; good blending coffee for all uses*
★	*fair*

FLAVOR PROFILE

Body	🫘🫘
Acidity	🫘🫘🫘🫘
Balance	🫘🫘🫘🫘

SURINAM

*An important name in the history
of the coffee.*

Surinam was the first country in South America to cultivate
coffee, and Norway was the main importer of the country's
production. Today, however, little is produced there, and the
country is included here for historical reasons only.

Etching of coffee gatherers on their way to work.

The Dutch, who had settled in Surinam in 1667, introduced the arabica tree in the early 18th century from Java,
and the first trees were presented by the burgomeister of
Amsterdam to a Flemish pirate, one Hansback, specifically to
plant in what was then Dutch Guyana. Coffee spread to
neighboring French Guyana a few years later when a French
criminal, Mourgues, was promised a pardon and a free passage to France if he introduced trees to the French colony,
which he duly did.

VENEZUELA

Wonderfully individual estate-grown coffees are coming from this oil-rich country.

Oil used to be thought of as Venezuela's chief export. In fact, although coffee trees were introduced from Martinique as early as 1730, coffee production was virtually abandoned during the oil boom. Recently, however, coffee farms – *fincas* – have begun to revive, and the old plantings of *tipica* and bourbon and new plantings are laying the basis of a new export industry. At present, most Venezuelan coffee is exported to Russia and to Colombia, where it is repacked. However, many of the small, recently re-established estates are beginning to export their coffee themselves.

The country's coffee industry is untypical in its complexity. There is no doubt that the best coffee-producing area is Tachira state, which is in the southwest, but unfortunately the name "Tachira" tends to be applied indiscriminately to beans from all over the country.

The best names to look out for are Montebello from San Cristóbal de Tachira; Miramar from Rubio de Tachira; Granija from Timote de Merida; Ala Granija from Santa Anna de Tachira. Other quality names are Maracaibos (which is actually the name of the port through which the coffee is exported); Merida and Trujillo; Santa Filomena; and Cucuta.

Among the estates in Merida, which is in the foothills of the Andes, is the one belonging to Pablo and Luisa Helena Pulido, which was one of the old farms that had been allowed to decline. Since they took it over in the early 1980s, the Pulido family has been harvesting coffee from the old bourbon plants as well as extending the farm with new plantings.

The area around Caracas, once famous for its coffee, is also being brought back into production, and another name to look out for is the coffee from *tipica* plants grown on the estate of Jean and Andres Boulton in Turgua.

The flavor of Venezuelan coffee is unlike any other from Latin America. It is light and delicate and has less acidity than is typical, which makes it useful for blending as well as being a flavorsome coffee in its own right.

FLAVOR	*good fruit flavors*
SUGGESTED ROAST	*medium to high; many uses*
★ ★	*good*

FLAVOR PROFILE

Body	🫘🫘🫘
Acidity	🫘🫘
Balance	🫘🫘🫘

Quality control and testing of blends in Kenya.

AFRICA

ANGOLA

An uncertain future for a once-great coffee producer.

In the mid-1970s, Angola exported over 3.5 million bags of coffee each year, of which 98 percent was robusta – and probably the best robusta to come from Africa. In 1990 the total production had declined to 200,000 bags.

The best known names from the past are Ambriz, Amborim, and Novo Redondo, which were renowned for their consistent quality. Most of the coffee was exported to the U.S. and to the Netherlands and, of course, to Portugal.

FLAVOR	*unavailable in the West for several years, but in the past was noted for high acidity*
SUGGESTED ROAST	*medium to dark*
★	*fair*

BURUNDI

Rich, soft coffee from a troubled area.

Burundi has one of the most diverse and, in its own way, one of the most successful coffee industries. It was introduced by Belgian colonizers as recently as 1930, and the coffee is grown on small farms. Unfortunately, many of these are on the border with war-torn Rwanda, which may lead to pressures on production.

Almost all of Burundi's coffee production is of arabica beans, and the trees in Ngozi are grown at altitudes over 4,000 feet. The coffee has excellent acidity and a very full aroma, and most of the production is exported to the U.S., Germany, Finland, and Japan.

FLAVOR PROFILE

Body	🫘🫘🫘🫘
Acidity	🫘🫘🫘🫘
Balance	🫘🫘🫘

FLAVOR	rich, aromatic coffee with high acidity
SUGGESTED ROAST	mid and high roast
★ ★	good

CAMEROON

A high-roast bean that is good in espresso.

The cultivation of arabica trees in Cameroon was begun in 1913, and the variety was Blue Mountain from Jamaica, but the country also produces equally large quantities of robusta coffee. The quality and character of the coffee used to be comparable with that from South America, with the best coffee coming from Bamileke and Bamoun in the northwest of the country. There is also some production of elephant bean and peaberry.

Recently there has been a decline in the quantity of coffee produced, with production of robusta falling from 1.8 million bags in 1987 to 1.1 million in 1990, and arabica declining from 400,000 to 200,000 bags in the same period. The powers of the National Coffee Supervisory Agency have been limited, which may result in an increase in both quality and quantity.

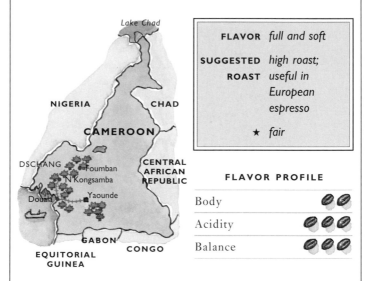

FLAVOR	full and soft
SUGGESTED ROAST	high roast; useful in European espresso
★	fair

FLAVOR PROFILE

Body	
Acidity	
Balance	

ETHIOPIA

In the beginning – was Ethiopia

The Arabica coffee tree originated in Ethiopia, where it grew wild – the name "coffee" derives from the Ethiopian town of Kaffa. In fact, many coffee trees still grow in the wild, and they produce coffee with a somewhat winy flavor and a heavy body. Man may first have learned how to cultivate the coffee tree in the 9th century, although who, how, and why remain mysteries. Local legend has it that coffee was first used by monks who needed to stay awake at night to pray.

Today Ethiopia is a significant producer, and quality Ethiopian coffees are among the most unusual in the world and are definitely worth seeking out. Some 12 million Ethiopians are dependent on the coffee industry, and Ethiopia is Africa's major exporter of arabica beans.

Traditional Ethiopian coffee ceremony.

All kinds of cultivation are found, from wild forest-grown trees and semi-developed plots, to traditionally run small plots to modern plantations. Approximately 50 percent of production is grown at over 5,000 feet above sea level.

A name to look out for is Harrar, for the coffee from this area is among the highest grown of all. Coffee from Harrar is classified as Shortberry and Longberry, and the Longberry is the most keenly sought. It has a soft, winy, almost gamey flavor with a memorable aroma, and it is lightly acidic. Another name to look for is Djimmah, where coffee grows wild at more than 4,000 feet and is sold as Lima and Babeka. Coffees from Sidamo, in the center of the country, which are marketed as Y (or Ygra) Chelfe, and from Lekempti, which have a particularly unusual flavor, are other names to remember. Do not be put off by the appearance of beans from Djimmah and Sidamo, which must be among the least attractive of beans – their flavor is excellent.

Perhaps the hardest of all Ethiopian beans to find are Yirgacheffes, which are exported to Japan and Europe, but are rarely seen in the U.S. This is because the Nestlé-owned German roaster, Dallmeyer, has developed a very close relationship with growers of the Yirgacheffes and usually has the largest single supply of these beans.

It is not easy to describe Ethiopian coffee. The flavor is not punchy or intense, nor does it have the acidity that one looks for in, for example, a Kenyan coffee. It should not be high roasted or it will lose its character.

The first famous coffee was Mocha (which is discussed in the entry for Yemen), and the character of both this and Ethiopian coffee is similar. Good Ethiopian stands comparison with the finest coffees from anywhere, and the best washed arabica beans will fetch premium prices.

Domestic consumption of coffee is the highest in Africa, and in the countryside it is often drunk with a herb known as the "health of Adam." The green beans are roasted over a fire; then they are pounded with the herb, and the whole concoction is brewed and drunk from very small cups, often as an accompaniment to a small pancake to which are added generous quantities of chilis.

The coffee industry is managed by the Ethiopian Coffee Marketing Corporation (ECMC), which controls about 90 percent of the export market. A few private export companies have always existed, even when the government was rigorously Marxist, and it seems likely that the hold of the ECMC will be loosened as the regions gain greater powers, and this movement seems likely to benefit the coffee industry as a whole and to the independent traders in particular. The coffee is sold at daily auction, and most is exported to Germany, the U.S., France, and Japan.

A problem facing the industry – one that has already caused serious disruption in Yemen – is proliferation of qat. Coffee plants have been left untended and even uprooted to make space for qat plants, so the recent rise in coffee prices has not come a moment too soon for the Ethiopian industry.

FLAVOR	*very unusual, rich, fruity, winy, gamey – must be tasted*
SUGGESTED ROAST	*medium*
★ ★ ★	*excellent*

FLAVOR PROFILE

Body	●
Acidity	● ● ● ●
Balance	● ● ● ● ●

IVORY COAST

Quantity rather than quality from one of the world's largest producers.

The Ivory Coast has never been a producer of the finest-quality coffee, and little of its output comes from arabica trees. The country is included here, however, because in the early 1980s it was the third largest producer in the world, with 5 million bags a year, and even now, a decade later, it is the fifth largest producer, at 4.4 million bags. In terms of production of robusta coffee, it is second only to Indonesia (with 6.8 million bags).

One of the causes for this decline is the fall in yield, which in the 1980s stood at 220 pounds per acre. This is partly because of the general poverty within the country and also partly because of the aging, and consequently less productive, trees. Lack of investment and a failure to provide long-term management structures have also affected the industry.

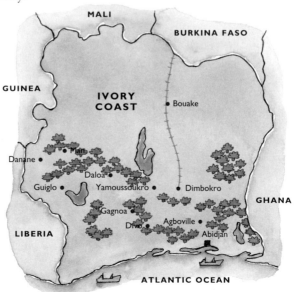

Drying coffee cherries in a village in the Ivory Coast.

The government has begun to take active steps to remedy the situation. The national regulatory board has been re-organized and slimmed down, and some of the production has been handed over to private companies. A minimum price is offered to farmers producing premium coffees, and exporters are being encouraged to buy direct from the farmer.

At present 80 percent of the exports find their way to the European Union, especially to France and Italy. If you drink a mass-market coffee in either of these countries, it is more than likely to contain coffee that originated in the Ivory Coast.

As a footnote it should be noted that the Ivory Coast is a major center for coffee smuggling, and as much as 26,000 tons were smuggled in 1993–4, mainly through neighboring Mali and Guinea.

FLAVOR	*full, soft flavor*
SUGGESTED ROAST	*dark*
★	*fair*

FLAVOR PROFILE

Body	🫘🫘🫘
Acidity	🫘🫘
Balance	🫘🫘🫘

KENYA

One of the finest coffees available – well known for its strong flavor, good aroma, and acidity.

Almost everyone who works in the coffee industry rates Kenyan coffee as one of their favorites. This is because Kenyan coffee has everything we want from a good cup of coffee. It has a wonderfully satisfying aroma, an excellent balance of acidity and body, and excellent fruit.

Coffee was introduced to Kenya in the 19th century, when Ethiopian coffee was imported into the country via South Yemen, but it was not until the early 20th century that bourbon trees were introduced by the St. Austin Mission.

Most Kenyan coffee grows at 5,000 to 7,000 feet, and there are two harvests each year. There may be as many as seven passes through the trees to make sure that only the mature berries are taken. The coffee is grown by smallholders, who deliver fresh cherries to cooperative washing stations, which then deliver the parchment coffee to cooperative unions (parchment is the last state of the coffee before dehusking).

Meryl Streep in OUT OF AFRICA *playing Karen Blixen on her coffee plantation in Kenya.*

All the coffee is pooled, so no estate-grown coffees are available, and the producer is paid the average price realized for each appropriate quality. This system generally works well and is fair to both producer and consumer.

The government takes the coffee industry extremely seriously. In fact, uprooting or otherwise destroying coffee trees is illegal. Buyers of Kenyan coffee are among the top coffee buyers in the world, and in recognition of this, no other country grows, produces, or markets its coffees as well or as consistently as Kenya. All the coffee beans are initially bought by the Coffee Board of Kenya (CBK), which tastes and grades the beans, which are then sold at weekly auctions, although they are ungraded when they are sold. The SBK acts as an agent only, holding the coffee samples and sending them out so that the buyers can judge the price and the quality. The Nairobi auctions are attended by private exporters, and the CBK pays the producer the price less a marketing charge. The best classifications are PB, Peaberry, then AA Plus-Plus, AA Plus, AA, AB, and so on down the scale. The best of the coffee is deliciously fragrant and has a bright, rather winy flavor.

The auctions are organized to meet the needs of the blenders. The lot sizes are small – 3–6 tons – and samples of each lot, together with the grower's mark, are available for tasting. After the auctions, exporters pack together the different styles, qualities, and quantities required by the blenders.

This permits great flexibility for the blenders, and the quality-conscious Germans and Scandinavians are among the regular buyers.

The rise of Kenyan coffee in international terms is obvious from the figures. In 1969–70, exports were 0.8 million bags; by 1985–6, that figure had peaked at 2 million bags. Production has now settled at 1.6 million bags, and the average yield is about 580 pounds per acre.

Even before the recent steep rise in coffee prices, the average price of Kenyan coffee had been increasing. Prices for 1993–4 were around 50 percent higher than those paid only 12 months before, and this rise was largely the result of increased demand.

Recently, however, some buyers, especially the Japanese, have expressed dissatisfaction with the Kenyan system. While the carefully regulated process might appear to be a model for all coffee-producing countries, some dealers have recently been expressing the view that quality has fallen and that buying direct from the farmers would be one way of improving the quality.

Kenyan coffee was promoted by Hollywood in the film *Out of Africa*, in which Meryl Streep plays the Danish writer and coffee farmer, Karen Blixen. Many people will probably remember the film for the breathtaking landscapes and spectacular sunsets, but others may remember it for the fantasies they had about having their own coffee plantation in Kenya.

FLAVOR	fragrant, sharp, fruity, and full
SUGGESTED ROAST	medium; the best can be high roasted
★ ★ ★	excellent

FLAVOR PROFILE

Body	🫘🫘🫘🫘
Acidity	🫘🫘🫘🫘🫘
Balance	🫘🫘🫘🫘🫘

Two of the best coffees from Kenya, AA (left) *and Peaberry* (right).

MADAGASCAR

Great things to come.

Madagascar is mainly a producer of robusta beans, but it has plans to increase the plantings of arabica.

Although the island is a one-party socialist republic, since 1989 the coffee industry has been privatized and freed from many regulations. Total production is high at around 1 million bags annually, but the domestic consumption is high because the Malagache are serious coffee-drinkers. France is the main export market, and the robusta is of excellent quality.

The government plans to develop about 5,000 acres of new robusta plantations and about 125,000 acres of arabica plantations, and the island's inclusion in this book is, therefore, largely on the basis of its potential as a producer of arabica, which, when fully underway, is expected to be of very good quality.

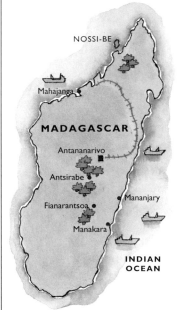

NOSSI-BE

Mahajanga

MADAGASCAR

Antananarivo

Antsirabe

Mananjary

Fianarantsoa

Manakara

INDIAN OCEAN

FLAVOR	fair acidity and balance
SUGGESTED ROAST	medium to dark; good for cappuccino
★ ★	good

FLAVOR PROFILE

Body	🫘🫘
Acidity	🫘🫘🫘
Balance	🫘🫘🫘🫘

MOZAMBIQUE

No coffee available from this war-torn country.

Political problems and internal strife have led to the virtual suspension of a once-thriving industry. Good-quality beans were produced in the Manica region in the center of the country, but no coffee is currently being exported from this unfortunate country.

RWANDA

A good-quality coffee from washed arabica beans with an unusual rich, full flavor.

Rwandan coffee production, in the form of washed arabica beans, was of extremely high quality, and the industry was notable, in African terms, in that the country strove only to produce the best possible beans.

The flavor of the coffee has been described as "grassy," a characteristic deriving from the tropical climate of the area. The soil is so rich and the climate so conducive to plant growth that the coffee is "forced" or "pressured" and often seems to have grown too fast to give the very top-rank beans. Nevertheless, the soft, rich flavor is extremely good.

FLAVOR	soft, rich, very full
SUGGESTED ROAST	high roast
★ ★	good

FLAVOR PROFILE

Body	🫘🫘🫘🫘
Acidity	🫘🫘
Balance	🫘🫘

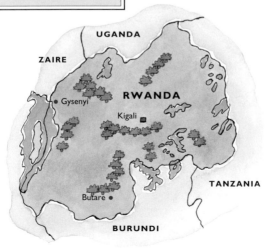

Napoleon thought that the only good thing to come from this tiny island was its coffee.

The island of St. Helena lies in the Atlantic Ocean, 1,200 miles from Africa and 2,200 miles from Brazil. It has a population of about 5,000, and it is, of course, famous as the island to which Napoleon was exiled in 1815 after the battle of Waterloo. He died there in 1821.

Coffee was first planted on the island in 1732, carried there on board the *Houghton* from Yemen. Although other plantings carried out in the 1860s failed, wild coffee trees grow on the island to this day.

The island is included here because it is about to undergo a coffee revolution. In the mid-1980s, David Henry began to develop the island's coffee industry with the aim of producing the best possible coffee. The trees are cultivated in a wholly organic way, and there is no mechanization – not even a tractor. Even the trees that are cut down to clear space for new coffee plantings are being recycled.

FLAVOR	rich, sweet coffee
SUGGESTED ROAST	light to medium
★ ★	good

FLAVOR PROFILE

Body	🫘🫘🫘
Acidity	🫘🫘🫘🫘
Balance	🫘🫘🫘

SAO TOMÉ AND PRINCIPE

A tiny production of top-quality arabica beans with a soft, full flavor.

The volcanic islands, which were a Portuguese colony until achieving their independence in 1975, are the second smallest independent country in Africa. The equator runs through the islands, making the climate hot and humid, but the soil is fertile and well drained, and coffee trees flourish there.

The arabica trees were introduced from Brazil in 1800, and 98 percent of production is still of arabica. However, only about 1,000 bags are exported each year, much of it going to quality-conscious consumers in Scandinavia.

FLAVOR	soft and full
SUGGESTED ROAST	high roast; a good blending coffee
★ ★	good

FLAVOR PROFILE

Body	🫘🫘🫘
Acidity	🫘🫘🫘
Balance	🫘🫘

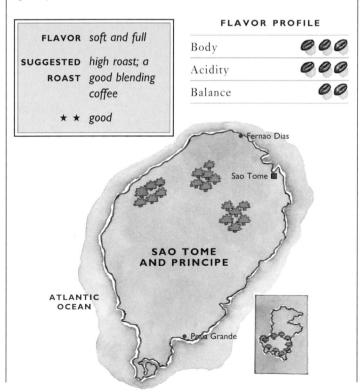

SAO TOME AND PRINCIPE

Fernao Dias

Sao Tome ■

ATLANTIC OCEAN

Praia Grande

SOUTH AFRICA

Fragrant coffee with less acidity, which is reminiscent of a Central American bean.

Coffee production in South Africa is concentrated in the northeast of the country, in Natal, between Lesotho and Mozambique, and further north in Transvaal. The southernmost limit is the 30th parallel; further south, the danger of frosts makes coffee production impossible.

The trees originated in Kenya, and the quality is excellent. In 1975 only about 400 acres were planted with coffee trees, but in 1987 a nine-year plan was introduced with the aim of bringing a further 2,400 acres under cultivation.

The coffee is interesting in that it is more like a bean from Central America than from Kenya, the source of the original plants. It is fragrant and pleasingly acidic.

FLAVOR	*rich with good acidity*
SUGGESTED ROAST	*low to medium roast*
★	*fair*

FLAVOR PROFILE

Body	🫘🫘🫘
Acidity	🫘🫘🫘
Balance	🫘🫘

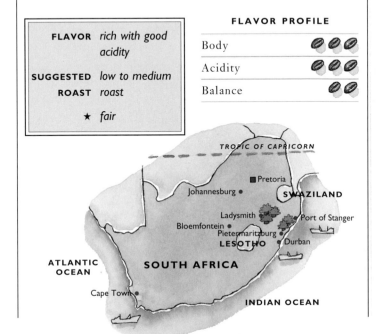

SUDAN

The civil war has all but killed coffee production.

The terrible civil war that has been waged on and off in the south of the country for the last 20 years has ruined the lives of millions of people and done untold damage to the countryside, including the coffee industry.

Robusta coffee is, or was, grown in the south, with arabica trees, which originally grew wild, planted in the north and east of the country.

Historically, the blacks from the south were taken as slaves by the Arabs, often to Arabia, and the slaves would take coffee cherries with them to sustain them during the journey. It was these beans that, according to tradition, became the arabica beans of Yemen, and it was these unfortunate Sudanese slaves who inadvertently initiated what is today the most widely grown and widely traded agricultural commodity in the world.

At present, the Sudanese coffee industry is, like the country, in a perilous state, and very little is being exported.

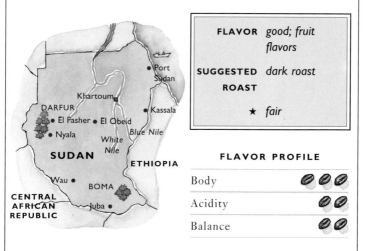

FLAVOR	good; fruit flavors
SUGGESTED ROAST	dark roast
★	fair

FLAVOR PROFILE

Body	🫘🫘🫘
Acidity	🫘🫘
Balance	🫘🫘

TANZANIA

*The best coffees are superb, with wonderfully soft
acidity and an excellent aroma.*

The coffees from Tanzania are an important export item in
the nation's economy. There is a good supply of peaberries,
which are said to have a more intense flavor than regular
beans, and generally the coffee has a bright, sharp character.
A good Tanzanian Chagga AA, for example, which comes
from the Moshi district near Mount Kilimanjaro, gives a
wonderfully full-bodied cup, with a superb fragrance.

The industry has suffered from political uncertainty, and
pests and diseases are rampant, leading to a lowering of overall standards and inconsistent quality. These problems have
led, in turn, to a fall in the price, which has had the usual

result of taking the industry still further downhill. In addition, it is estimated that between 1969 and 1985 around 12 percent of the fine-quality arabica grown in northern Tanzania was smuggled into Kenya. However, of late there have been signs of improvement – slow, to be sure, but nevertheless welcome – for at its best Tanzanian coffee ranks among the finest.

In the past, the industry was dominated by estate-grown coffees, but now more than 85 percent is produced by small-holders, many of whom are organized into cooperatives. The most important group of growers is the Kilimanjaro Cooperative Union (KNUC). Coffee is sold at auction to private exporters by the Tanzanian Coffee Marketing Board (TCMB). During the 1980s, much of the country's production was diverted from the auctions and sold directly to the TCMB, but this has been changed. The coffee industry is being liberated so that in the future private individuals and groups will be allowed to buy coffee, which will be graded in a different way, to encourage buyers from Germany, Finland, the Netherlands, Belgium, and Japan.

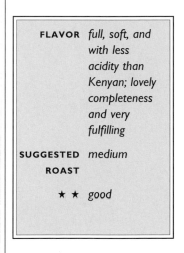

FLAVOR	*full, soft, and with less acidity than Kenyan; lovely completeness and very fulfilling*
SUGGESTED ROAST	*medium*
★ ★	*good*

FLAVOR PROFILE

Body	🫘🫘🫘🫘🫘
Acidity	🫘🫘
Balance	🫘🫘🫘🫘

Tanzanian Kibo Chagga, appreciated by connoisseurs.

163

UGANDA

High hopes for the future.

The production of arabica accounts for only 10 percent of the country's total coffee, but it is well worth looking out for. The best of the coffee is grown in the northeast, along the Kenyan border in the area of Mount Elgon and Bugisu, and in the west in the area of Mount Ruwensori. It becomes available for export in January or February.

The equator passes through Uganda, and the resulting climate has made this country one of the world's main producers of robusta beans. In the 1960s, coffee production stood at 3.5 million bags per year, but largely because of political problems, this had fallen to around 2.5 million bags in the mid-1980s. Now, however, coffee production has risen again and currently stands at about 3 million bags.

Sorting coffee beans in Uganda.

One of the major problems facing the industry has been the lack of good roads along which the coffee can be transported to the ports of Mombasa in Kenya or Dar es Salaam in Tanzania.

The monopoly of the Coffee Marketing Board (CMB) was ended in November 1990 in an attempt to improve quality and reduce costs. Cooperatives now do most of the work previously carried out by the CMB. The privatized industry now produces approximately two-thirds of the country's export earnings, but this led the government to impose a tax on coffee in the hope that it would generate much-needed income. Instead it has led to a 20 percent drop in coffee exports and an increase in coffee smuggling.

As in Tanzania, the recent rise in coffee prices has encouraged coffee farmers to return to their plantations, and it is hoped that much of the once-abandoned land will be brought back into cultivation.

FLAVOR	*full, rich coffee; very complete cup satisfaction*
SUGGESTED ROAST	*medium to high*
★ ★	*good*

FLAVOR PROFILE

Body	🫘🫘🫘🫘
Acidity	🫘🫘🫘🫘
Balance	🫘🫘🫘🫘🫘

YEMEN

*Medium-roast beans with a gamey flavor come
from the home of coffee.*

Even before the 6th century, Yemen was called Arabia and
the trees that were sent out from here were known as "arabica,"
even though the original source of the plants was Ethiopia.
The Dutch were responsible for the dispersal of coffee trees
throughout the world. Dutch traders traveling east around the
Cape of Good Hope sailed up the east coast of Africa as far
as the port of Mocha before they set out on their distant
journey to the Indies. In 1696 the Dutch took plants to
Ceylon, where plants had already been introduced by Arabs,
perhaps as early as 1500, and then on to Batavia in Java.

Mocha coffee beans are smaller and more rounded than
most, which makes them look like a peaberry bean – in fact,
peaberry beans were sometimes called "Mocha." The finest
Mocha is like a Harrar bean from Ethiopia. It has a light body
and high acidity, like Kenyan coffee, but combined with an
almost indescribably exotic pungency. The flavor is traditionally a little gamey and chocolatey, and the practice of adding
chocolate to coffee was a natural development.

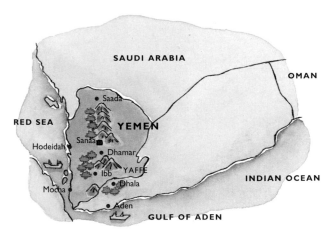

In Yemen poplar trees are planted to provide the coffee trees with the shade they need. They are grown, as they were in the past, on steep terraces to make the most of the low rainfall and lack of suitable land. In addition to Typica and Bourbon plants, about 10 local varieties, descended from the original beans from Ethiopia, are still grown. Even the finest grades, such as Mocha Extra, are dried with the fruit still attached to the bean. The dried husks are often still removed in the traditional way between millstones, which not only makes the beans into irregular shapes, but frequently damages them.

Although Yemeni coffee can be excellent, soft, and aromatic at its best, unfortunately consistent quality cannot be guaranteed. The grading of the beans is erratic, although traditionally the best comes from Mattari, with that from Sharki next best, followed by Sanani. The beans, which are naturally low in caffeine, are available for export between December and April. In the past, there have been problems with coffee from the north being adulterated before it was shipped through the southern port of Aden. Only coffee shipped through the port of Hodeida can be definitely regarded as being from the north. Largely because of lack of funds on the part of the growers, the coffee is largely organic.

"Baghdad Boiler" — mid-17th century copper-plated coffee kettle.

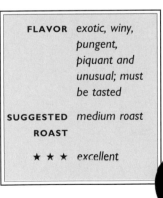

FLAVOR	exotic, winy, pungent, piquant and unusual; must be tasted
SUGGESTED ROAST	medium roast
★ ★ ★	excellent

FLAVOR PROFILE

Body	
Acidity	
Balance	

ZAÏRE

Arabica beans used to have a high reputation for quality and quantity.

The best Zaïrean coffee is grown in the northeast of the country, especially in the provinces of Oriental and Kivu, and these areas used to produce some of the best peaberry and elephant beans. Sadly, top-quality coffee from Zaïre is becoming increasingly rare. When it can be found, however, Zaïrean coffee is the perfect cup. Like Kenyan coffee, it produces an ideal balance of acidity, body, and aroma.

The industry has recently been privatized, and it is to be hoped that the recent rise in prices will help to provide the investment that is necessary to revive the industry. Approximately 16,000 acres are planted with arabica beans and 89,000 acres of robusta. Before independence in 1960, most production was on estates, and when world coffee prices slumped in 1989, many farmers abandoned their farms. Now the coffee is largely grown on numerous smallholdings.

FLAVOR	good, acidic coffee; useful for blending
SUGGESTED ROAST	medium to high
★	fair

FLAVOR PROFILE

Body	🫘🫘🫘
Acidity	🫘🫘🫘🫘
Balance	🫘🫘🫘

ZAMBIA

A coffee that is a little lighter than Kenyan and that should be drunk later in the day.

Coffee was brought to Zambia from Kenya and Tanzania in the early years of the 20th century, and both elephant and peaberry beans are available.

The top-quality Zambian coffees are good tending to excellent, with a taste somewhat similar to, though lighter than, Kenyan coffee, which it equals in price. It is grown in two areas in the north around Kasama, and in Nakonde and Isoka districts as well as near the capital Lusaka.

FLAVOR	*full; good for blending*
SUGGESTED ROAST	*high roast, good for espresso*
★ ★	*good*

FLAVOR PROFILE

Body	●●●
Acidity	●●●
Balance	●●●

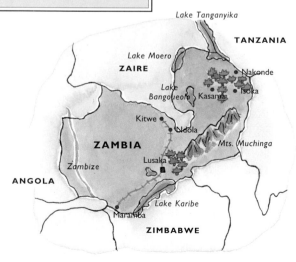

169

ZIMBABWE

Good-quality arabica beans supplying the gourmet trade.

Coffee cultivation began comparatively recently, in the 1960s, when farmers from South Africa established coffee plantations. Zimbabwe's coffee production is concentrated in the country's Eastern Highlands, near to the border with Mozambique. The highlands are dominated by the Chimanimani range and, further north, by the Nyanga Mountains, which are overshadowed by Mount Inyangani. The main growing area is around the town of Chipinge, at the southern end of the Eastern Highlands.

One of the most interesting of the coffee producers is the Farfell Coffee Estate, a small, family concern, producing strictly high-grown, hand-picked, sun-dried beans. The estate has almost 420 acres of arabica trees, which thrive in the good soil, high altitude and regular rain, and it aims to produce fine, gourmet-quality coffee.

In general, Zimbabwean coffee is similar to, and every bit as good as, Kenyan AA, offering a soft, clean, fruit taste.

FLAVOR	full, soft, clean with good fruit
SUGGESTED ROAST	medium
	★ ★ good

FLAVOR PROFILE

Body	● ● ●
Acidity	● ● ● ●
Balance	● ● ●

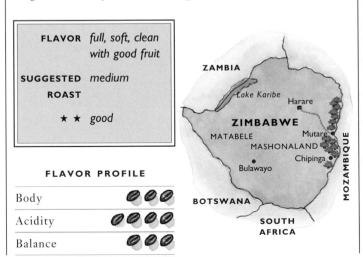

Picking cherries in Taiwan.

ASIA AND THE
INDIAN OCEAN

CHINA

Coffee in the home of tea.

The question that once puzzled coffee professionals was whether coffee was actually grown in China.

China does, in fact, export coffee, and coffee trees are known to grow there. However, no one knows for sure how many trees there are and how much coffee they produce, for no production statistics are available. It seems possible that at least some of the coffee exported from China is in reality re-exported Tanzanian coffee.

The country is now, however, a net importer, and it is becoming so popular that it is even being advertised on television. This entry appears, therefore, on the basis of China's re-exported coffee and because the country is a future major consumer.

FLAVOR	*acceptable*
SUGGESTED ROAST	*light to mid*
★	*fair*

FLAVOR PROFILE

Body	●●
Acidity	●●●
Balance	●●

INDIA

Coffees with a delicate hint of spice, and good body.

Indian coffee is of interest to coffee-lovers for several reasons, but the most important is the process, applied to some beans, that is known as "monsooning." In the days when goods and people were transported to and from India under sail, it could take a ship several months to travel to Europe. During the journey the green beans were exposed to high levels of humidity, and this changed both their flavor and their color, until by the journey's end they had turned from green to a curious shade of yellow.

Customers became used to this, and when steamships shortened the journey time, coffee producers found that their customers still wanted the color and flavor of the voyage-affected beans. In order to reproduce these characteristics, the process of "monsooning" was introduced. The monsoon occurs in the southwest of India in May and June, and during this period the beans are spread, to a depth of 5 to 8 inches in special open-sided buildings, where they are left for five

days and raked over from time to time so that all the beans are exposed to the air, which has an unusually high degree of humidity at this time. The beans are then loosely packed into bags and stacked so that the monsoon winds can blow around and over the sacks. The sacks are repacked and restacked once a week for seven weeks, until the beans have changed flavor and color. Finally, the beans are hand-filtered to remove any that have been unaffected by "monsooning," and they are then packed for export. Supplies of monsoon coffee are available from October to February.

In addition to Karnataka, good-quality coffee is also grown at Tellichery and Malabar in Kerala state, also in the southwest, and Nilgiris in Tamil Nadu state (formerly Madras state) in the southeast.

Good-quality Indian coffee is classified as Arabica Plantation, of which the best grades are A, B, C, and T. Monsoon coffees are classified as Monsooned Malabar AA and Monsooned Basanically. There is also some peaberry production. The problems facing the coffee industry are largely those currently facing the country as a whole – too much bureaucracy, overtaxation, and lack of investment. At present, the Indian Coffee Board controls the industry and collects the beans for sale. The coffee is then sold at auction in large lots, which are combined together to create commercial-sized quantities that do not, unfortunately, allow for estate and regional differences to be preserved. Many good producers, therefore, lack sufficient incentive to produce beans of individual character or exceptional quality. An attempt to overcome this problem was made in 1992, with the production of Valley Nuggets from Plantation grade A beans from separate good-quality areas, and it is to be hoped that this will encourage other growers, for there is certainly a desire among many growers to enter the gourmet coffee market.

FLAVOR	smooth, rich, spicy, full bodied
SUGGESTED ROAST	medium
★ ★	good

FLAVOR PROFILE

Body	🫘🫘🫘🫘
Acidity	🫘
Balance	🫘🫘

INDONESIA

Refreshing and full-bodied, this coffee is good at any time of the day.

Coffee is produced throughout the Indonesia archipelago, and Java is one of the great names of coffee history.

The trees were introduced to Indonesia by the Dutch in the mid-17th century (some authorities think it was earlier than this), and the first coffee from Java was sold in Amsterdam in 1712. However, in 1877, all the plantations were wiped out by coffee rust, and robusta trees were imported from Africa to replace the old trees. Today, only 6 to 10 percent of the total coffee production is of arabica beans, and Indonesia is the world's major producer of robusta, with 6.8 million bags annually. Most of the coffee is produced on small plantations, which account for about 90 percent of the total production.

The best growing areas throughout the archipelago are on Java, Sumatra, Sulawesi, and Flores. East Timor was a major producer of excellent coffee until its annexation by Indonesia.

Java produces a subtly aromatic coffee that, with its relatively low acidity, is smooth and pleasantly balanced. It is more acidic than the coffee from Sumatra or Sulawesi and has a spicier flavor. The best estates are Blawan, Jambit, Kayumas, and Pankur. Mocha Java is a blend of Java and mocha coffee from the Yemen.

Cherry pickers in Indonesia after a day's work.

FLAVOR	Sumatra is heavy bodied, broody, syrupy and chocolatey (ideal for after dinner); Java is more earthy, spicier, full bodied, and with mid acidity
SUGGESTED ROAST	dark medium to dark; good espresso single or blend; excellent in a lattè
★ ★ ★	excellent

FLAVOR PROFILE

Body	🫘🫘🫘🫘🫘
Acidity	🫘🫘
Balance	🫘🫘

Sumatra, the second largest of the islands, is the center of the Indonesian oil industry and numbers rubber and hardwood among its best-known exports. However, Sumatran coffee, which is similar to Java coffee although the Indonesian beans give a rather heavier body, is preferred by many connoisseurs. The Mandheling and Ankola beans are especially highly regarded, and the beans from Mandheling have even been described as the most full-bodied arabica in the world.

Sulawesi, which lies between Borneo and New Guinea, is also sometimes called the Celebes. Its full-bodied Indonesian coffee has a rich flavor and splendid aroma. The best-known beans are from Kalossi in the south of the island – among labeled brands, look out for Celebes Kalossi – and from Rantepao.

One of the leading producers on New Guinea is the Sigri Estate, which, like the island as a whole, produces full-bodied, well-balanced coffee.

Indonesian coffee as a whole is quite strong and warmly flavored, with a rather syrupy quality and often with excellent acidity. Two of the main export markets are Germany and Japan, which is an indication of the high quality of the coffee. At their best, the arabicas are superb, with a richness that is characteristic of the bean. If you take milk or cream in your coffee, you can add it to a top-quality Indonesian arabica coffee without fear of affecting the flavor. There are six grades, the best being AP, although no one is certain what the initials stand for.

Coffee from these islands suffered the same problems as Indian coffee from Mysore when steamships took over from sail – that is, the customers had grown so used to the effects of the passage on the coffee bean that they were unwilling to accept the "fresher" product. To overcome this, and in an attempt to replicate the conditions produced by the long voyage, the Indonesian government kept the beans in "go-downs" for over a year. Unfortunately, the flavor of these sweated coffees was not widely acceptable, and the popularity of both Java and Sumatra began to wane.

Indonesian "passage" or "go-down" coffee, with its individual flavor, is still produced. It is sold under the trade names Old Government, Old Brown and Old Java.

Curiously, Indonesians themselves prefer to drink coffee in the Turkish, not the European, style.

Sorting beans in East Java, Indonesia.

LA RÉUNION

The home of the bourbon arabica no longer.

In 1715, the first 40 coffee trees were taken to the island of La Réunion from Mocha in Yemen. Unfortunately, only two trees survived the journey, but by 1719, the plantation had prospered and the first sale of beans was held. The next few years saw the government take a resolute, not to say robust, approach to coffee: it promulgated a law by which every inhabitant of the island, black and white, was obliged to plant 100 coffee trees every year. In 1723 the law was amended to specify that all slaves had to plant 200 mocha coffee trees and that anyone who destroyed a coffee tree should be executed.

At this time the island, a French colony, was known as Bourbon – a name shared with the coffee produced there and the species of arabica plants that were re-exported from there to other countries.

It is ironic that today the bourbon arabica coffee tree is widely planted and appreciated throughout the world, yet there is little or no coffee production in La Réunion itself. Below are characteristics of the bourbon variety in general.

FLAVOR	*rich; full of snap*
SUGGESTED ROAST	*medium to dark*
★ ★	*good*

FLAVOR PROFILE

Body	🫘🫘🫘
Acidity	🫘🫘
Balance	🫘🫘🫘

PHILIPPINES

A great future.

Coffee was introduced into the Philippines in the early 18th century, and by 1880 the country was the fourth largest exporter of coffee in the world. Coffee leaf rust had such a devastating effect, however, that soon after 1880, the country became a net importer.

Production has been revived, however, and today, after somewhat slow progress, the country has a growing and potentially good-quality coffee industry. The industry is run, rather loosely, by the national department of trade and industry, although all exports are carried out by private companies.

The Philippines are, in fact, one of the very few producers to grow all four varieties of coffee – robusta, liberica, excelsa, and arabica. The island of Maintain, the second largest and most southerly of the major islands in the group, produces high-grown arabicas of the highest quality.

FLAVOR	mild; quite full; some spiciness
SUGGESTED ROAST	mid to high; good for espresso blends
★	fair

FLAVOR PROFILE

Body	🫘🫘🫘
Acidity	🫘🫘🫘
Balance	🫘🫘🫘🫘

179

No coffee available outside Taiwan.

This is, perhaps, the strangest entry in the book. There used to be around 740 acres of coffee trees in Taiwan, but all the production was consumed locally.

At present, however, the success of gourmet coffee within Taiwan is a good indication that coffee can flourish in this region for the long term. Coffeeshops in Taiwan have become fashionable, upscale meeting places, and their popularity has increased since the early 1980s. They offer menu-style selections of coffees from all over the world, and the Cona method of preparation is very popular.

Cherry picking in Taiwan.

VIETNAM

A large producer today – a potential giant tomorrow.

It is, perhaps, typical of the French that they planted trees wherever their colonial influence was felt. Arabica trees were first brought to Vietnam by French missionaries, and between 1865 and 1876 more than 400,000 coffee trees, mostly from Java or Bourbon (La Réunion), were planted around Tonkin.

Today, coffee production is low but increasing. Vietnam is already an important exporter of tea, and coffee could well be next on the list. The production is mainly of robusta beans, and progress has been swift. In 1982, 66,000 bags were exported; in 1994 this had risen to over 200,000 tons. Of this quantity of robusta, 96 percent comes from small farms, although some state farms also have coffee trees.

Yields can be as high as 2,000 pounds per acre, and Japanese investment lies behind much of the new plantings.

FLAVOR	mid range; good balance
SUGGESTED ROAST	mid to high; good blending coffee for all uses
★	fair

FLAVOR PROFILE

Body	🫘🫘
Acidity	🫘🫘🫘
Balance	🫘🫘🫘

Top-quality coffee from Hawaii.

Australia
and the
Pacific Rim

AUSTRALIA

An opportunity to taste Australia's coffee should never be declined.

Australia is a surprising country in many ways, and perhaps one of the most surprising aspects is the high-quality coffee that is produced there.

Australian coffee, which is made entirely from the arabica bourbon variety, is of a very high quality. The flavor is soft, with unusually little bitterness or caffeine. Unfortunately, only small amounts find their way onto the export market, for production is limited by high labor costs and, perhaps surprisingly, by the high levels of sunshine. It is too hot to use the cheaper, mechanical pickers, and the coffee has to be harvested by hand, which tends to push up the production costs.

FLAVOR	*fun, with good acidity*
SUGGESTED ROAST	*medium*
★ ★	*good*

FLAVOR PROFILE

Body	●●
Acidity	●●●●
Balance	●●●

Hawaii

Is this the most beautiful coffee bean in the world?

The Kona bean has more luster and is more perfectly proportioned than any other coffee bean. The flavor is rich, almost nutty, and is unusually full-bodied, with a fine aroma. Some tasters detect cinnamon tones in the smooth, even flavor. Kona coffee may truly be described as luscious.

It is the only top-quality coffee to be produced within the fifty states, and the largest market is, naturally, to the U.S. mainland. Among all coffee producers, the Hawaiian industry is among the most tightly regulated and has the highest labor costs, although it does enjoy the best investment levels.

The coffee trees in Hawaii have to compete for space with the demands of the tourist industry, and the coffee is actually grown on the slopes of Mauna Loa, a volcano in the western Kona district of the island of Hawaii, in an area about 20 miles long, with production concentrated in the north and south of the region, but not in the center. The trees were planted in the inhospitable, yet rich, lava on the volcano's slopes. Although the initial planting was a labor-intensive, difficult operation, the trees in Kona, at least those growing above 300 feet, do not seem to suffer from any disease.

Despite the tornadoes to which the Hawaiian islands are periodically subject, the climatic conditions would seem to be almost perfect for coffee-growing – the right amounts of rain and sun and no frost. In addition, there is a curious local phenomenon, known as "free shade." It seems that on most days, at about 2 o'clock in the afternoon, clouds appear and provide the coffee trees with some welcome shade. So good are the conditions, in fact, that the Kona produces the highest yield of any arabica plantation in the world, while still maintaining its high quality. The average production in Latin America, for example, is 500 to 800 pounds per acre; at Kona, the production averages 2,000 pounds per acre. Unfortunately for coffee-lovers, however, there are only about 3,000 acres producing Kona coffee.

True Kona is not easy to find. The best Kona coffee is classified as Extra Fancy, Fancy, and Number One, with estate- and organically grown coffees also available. Much of the coffee claiming to be "Kona" contains less than 5 percent true Hawaiian Kona. An alternative brand to search for is Hawaii Kai Farms, which is available.

FLAVOR	smooth, intense aroma, nutty, luscious
SUGGESTED ROAST	light to medium
★ ★ ★	excellent

FLAVOR PROFILE

Body	🫘🫘🫘🫘
Acidity	🫘🫘
Balance	🫘🫘🫘🫘

A choice of styles available from Kona.

NEW CALEDONIA

Shades of past glories.

Only 10 percent of the land of this former French colony is capable of cultivation, but until recent political problems disrupted the economy, coffee vied with maize as the main crop.

Missionaries introduced coffee from La Réunion in 1860, but by 1987 only 40 tons were being produced annually, of which 37 tons were exported, mostly to France. The beans are an unusual robusta with an excellent, full-bodied flavor. It is, however, rather delicate and should be only lightly roasted.

New Caledonia is included here as a reminder of past delights and in the hope that future coffee-drinkers will be able to sample the classic taste.

CORAL SEA

NEW CALEDONIA

Touho · Ponerihouen
Heinghene · Canala
Gomen · Kone · Bourail · Maindoa · Bouralee
Vah

FLAVOR	silky; well balanced
SUGGESTED ROAST	light to light-medium
★ ★	good

FLAVOR PROFILE

Body	🫘🫘🫘🫘
Acidity	🫘🫘🫘
Balance	🫘🫘🫘🫘

The backdrop for a great modern coffee romance.

About 75 percent of the production comes from small, native farms, many in forest clearings and some so deep in the forests that they are almost inaccessible. The coffee is almost entirely high grown, being produced at altitudes between 4,265 and 5,905 feet above sea level, and its high quality is largely due to the altitudes at which so much of it is grown. There is comparatively little lowland, although robusta beans are grown in some low-lying areas. In addition, most of the native-grown coffees are organic, simply because of the problems and cost of transporting fertilizers and pesticides to the farms.

Coffee is a significant element in the country's economy, with over a million people involved, directly or indirectly. The government supports the farmers by offering a minimum price at the beginning of each season, and the industry itself is controlled by the Coffee Industry Board, which is based in Goroka in the east of the island. Exports, however, are in the hands of private companies.

The frost that destroyed so much of Brazil's crop in 1975 helped to expand coffee production in Papua New Guinea. The government of Papua New Guinea introduced a scheme

whereby village or group landowners would be sponsored to establish plantations of about 50 acres, and this measure did much to increase the penetration of coffee cultivation in the local economy – to such an extent that, by 1990, production was standing at 1 million bags a year.

Almost inevitably, however, this overproduction resulted in a lack of quality control. Until 1991 the basic bean was known as Y grade, but quality had deteriorated so much that European buyers had stopped buying the beans. There had also been a gradual erosion in the premium price that Y-grade beans had once commanded and that was linked to the country's policy of "one price, one grade" – a policy that, in an industry such as coffee in which quality is variable, is wholly unsustainable. As a result, poor-quality beans had corrupted the generally high standard of Y-grade production, and it became unsaleable.

The government's solution was to create new quality grades and to put a virtual end to the production of Y-grade coffee and the "one price, one grade policy." This allowed buyers to pay premium prices for better-quality beans, which had the inevitable effect on the income of the less-quality-conscious farmers. By 1993 the problem was more or less over, and most of the traditional buyers, including Jacob Suchard, have begun buying from Papua New Guinea again. Y grade is also now selling again at a slight premium, indicating that its quality has improved.

Although some of the native coffees are exciting, they are inconsistent. The harvested beans tend to be of diverse maturity and size, which makes them something of a lottery. Of the top grades, AA is rare, while A and AB are more widely obtainable. The mainstream production of a grade-A plantation, however, will have full body, fairly light acidity, and a little ranginess, together with great character.

FLAVOR	gamey; rich; full bodied; rangy
SUGGESTED ROAST	medium to high; excellent for blending
★ ★	good

FLAVOR PROFILE

Body	@ @ @ @
Acidity	@ @
Balance	@ @ @

TAHITI

Coffee from Paradise.

You will be very fortunate if you chance upon Tahitian coffee, because it is extremely difficult to find.

The commercial name is Tahiti Arabica, and it is unusual for any coffee to be exported from this, the largest of the Society Islands. If you do taste it, you will find it has a good, rounded flavor and a lot of personality.

FLAVOR	good; rounded; spicy acidity; good balance
SUGGESTED ROAST	medium
★ ★	good

FLAVOR PROFILE

Body	🫘🫘🫘
Acidity	🫘🫘
Balance	🫘🫘🫘🫘

U.S. MAIL-ORDER COFFEE HOUSES

Allegro Coffee
1930 Central Avenue
Boulder, CO 80301
Tel: 1–800 666 4869
    (303) 444 4844

Armeno Coffee Roasters Ltd.
75 Otis St.
Northborough, MA 01532
Tel: 1–800 276 3661
    (508) 393 2821

Berres Brothers Coffee
101 Western Ave.
Watertown, WI 53094
Tel: 1–800 233 5443
    (414) 261 6158

Blue Moon Espresso
1115 Wilson Boulevard
Arlington, VA 22209
Tel: (703) 527 7020

Cocoa Beach Coffee Co.
P.O. Box 112516
Tacoma, WA 98411
Tel: 1–800 755 9497
    (206) 925 5944

Coffee Connection
6 Drydock Avenue
Boston, MA 02210
Tel: (617) 261 4800

Community Kitchens Coffee
The Art of Food Plaza
Ridgely, MD 21685
Tel: 1–800 535 9901

Green Mountain Coffee Roasters
33 Coffee Lane
Waterbury, VT 05676
Tel: 1–800 223 6768

Peet's Coffee and Tea
PO Box 8247
Emeryville, CA 94662
Tel: 1–800 999 2132
    (415) 221 8506

Seattle's Best Coffee
1530 Post Alley
Seattle, WA 98101
Tel: 1–800 243 5206
    (206) 467 7700

Starbucks Coffee
2203 Airport Way South
PO Box 34510
Seattle, WA 98124–1510
Tel: 1–800 782 7282
    (206) 447 7950

Tully's Coffee Corp.
2010 Airport Way South
Seattle, WA 98134
Tel: (206) 233 2070

INDEX

PICTURE CREDITS

Bramah Tea and Coffee Museum: pp9, 49, 53, 54, 57, 58, 60, 61, 167; BFI Stills, Posters and Designs: p153; Courtesy Coffee & Cocoa International: pp106, 165; Gregory K. Clark Photographics: pp44, 68, 77, 90, 95, 99, 148, 171; The International Coffee Organization: pp7, 18, 20, 21, 22, 23, 24, 25, 27, 28, 30, 31, 32 (top and bottom), 34, 41, 79, 101, 110, 119, 125, 128, 129, 132, 176, 177; The Mansell Collection: pp6, 10, 17, 140;

Retrograph Archive Ltd: © pp1, 12, 69, 81, 86, 130.

The Publishers would also like to thank the following for their help in the preparation of this book:

Algerian Coffee Stores Ltd, Bramah Tea and Coffee Museum, The Edmonds Group (coffee and tea merchants), Fairfax Engineering Limited, H. R. Higgins Ltd, and Lavazza Coffee (UK) Limited.